CRADLES OF CIVILIZATION

**Ancient Egypt
and early Middle Eastern civilizations**

Devised and produced by
Andrea Dué
Text by
Renzo Rossi

MACMILLAN LIBRARY REFERENCE USA
NEW YORK

INTRODUCTION

First published in Italian by Jaca Book
© Editoriale Jaca Book Spa, Milano
1993

This edition published 1996
by Macmillan Library Reference USA
866 Third Avenue
New York, NY 10022

English Language Translation
Copyright © Simon and Schuster
Macmillan 1996

Text by Renzo Rossi
Scientific adviser Jean-Daniel Forest
Translation by Patricia Borlenghi
Edited by Brian Williams
Maps and plans and models by
Alessandro Bartolozzi,
Roberto Simoni, Chiara Pignaris,
Carla Angelozzi, Elizabetta Giuliani
Colour illustrations by Roberto Simoni,
Giorgio Bacchin, Giuseppe Cicio,
Paolo Ravaglia, Alessandro Bartolozzi,
Rosanna Rea
Black and white illustrations by
Chiara Pignaris, Roberto Simoni
Produced by AS Publishing

Library of Congress Cataloging-in-
Publication Data

Rossi, Renzo, 1940-
    [Atlanti della storia dell'uomo.
English]
    The atlas of human history/devised
and produced by Andrea Dué; text by
Renzo Rossi.
        p.; cm.
        Includes indexes.
        Contents: [1] The first people – [2]
The first settlers – [3] Cradles of
civilization – [4] The first Europeans –
[5] Civilizations of Asia – [6]
Civilizations of the Americas.
    ISBN 0-02-860285-4 (v. 1). –
    ISBN 0-02-860286-2 (v. 2). –
    ISBN 0-02-860287-0 (v. 3). –
    ISBN 0-02-860288-9 (v. 4) –
    ISBN 0-02-860289-7 (v. 5). –
    ISBN 0-02-860290-0 (v. 6)
    1. History, Ancient – Maps for
children. 2. Historical geography –
Maps for children. 3. Children's atlases.
[1. Civilization, Ancient – Maps.
2. Historical geography – Maps.
3. Atlases.]
    I. Dué, Andrea. II. Title.
G1033.R6 1996 <G&M>
930–dc20   95-8622
                                         CIP
                                    MAP AC

Printed and bound in Italy by Grafiche
Editoriali Padane Spa, Cremona

Human history is marked by a number of events which, with hindsight, appear quite revolutionary. One of these major stages occurred in the Middle East when almost simultaneously city-states grew up over a relatively short period of time in Mesopotamia and Egypt.

Simple farming communities were transformed into vast, organized societies that had all the characteristics of distinct civilizations. People congregated in densely packed centres with rulers, priests and officials to regulate and organize their activities. Writing and number systems developed to cope with the mass of complicated business to be transacted. As a result of trade, people grew rich, and the richest formed an élite from which the officials were chosen. They used their wealth to build palaces and temples, which were decorated and furnished in great style. Art flourished in a spectacular way.

This spontaneous development of art occurred, with no obvious outside influences, in only a few places on earth – Mesopotamia, Egypt, the Indus Valley, China, Central America and Peru. Only through the work of archaeologists do we know about these 'hotspots', for they all occurred in ancient times before there were written records. Written records from the same civilizations have been found, but these are from later periods than those from which the earliest art dates. Writing began in the Middle East about 3000 BC. During the last century, archaeologists have found a wealth of evidence, including written documents, from tombs, temples and many other buildings that enable us to build a picture of the way people lived. The civilizations of Mesopotamia and Egypt grew and spread over a long period. Their cultures influenced many others around them at the time and down the ages, so that even today their influence is ever-present in Western civilization, having been passed on to us by the civilizations of Greece and Rome.

The Sumerian civilization began around 3500 BC with the growth of farming communities on the fertile plains of the Tigris and Euphrates rivers. Food was plentiful, so there was time for crafts and for seeking new materials and new people to trade with along the rivers. As the Sumerians moved into new territory they met settlers with cultures less developed than their own. Sometimes the encounters would be peaceful, and the people ready to admire and benefit from the newcomers' superior skills. Sometimes the encounters were hostile and violent, so that the Sumerians had to fight to hold on to their position of power.

This happened with most of the ancient civilizations. As they grew and spread, they had to defend themselves against peoples around them who were less developed and always ready to attack them. In time, the civilization would outgrow its strength and deteriorate, allowing other cultures to take over and continue the development, or let it die.

B.W.

Contents

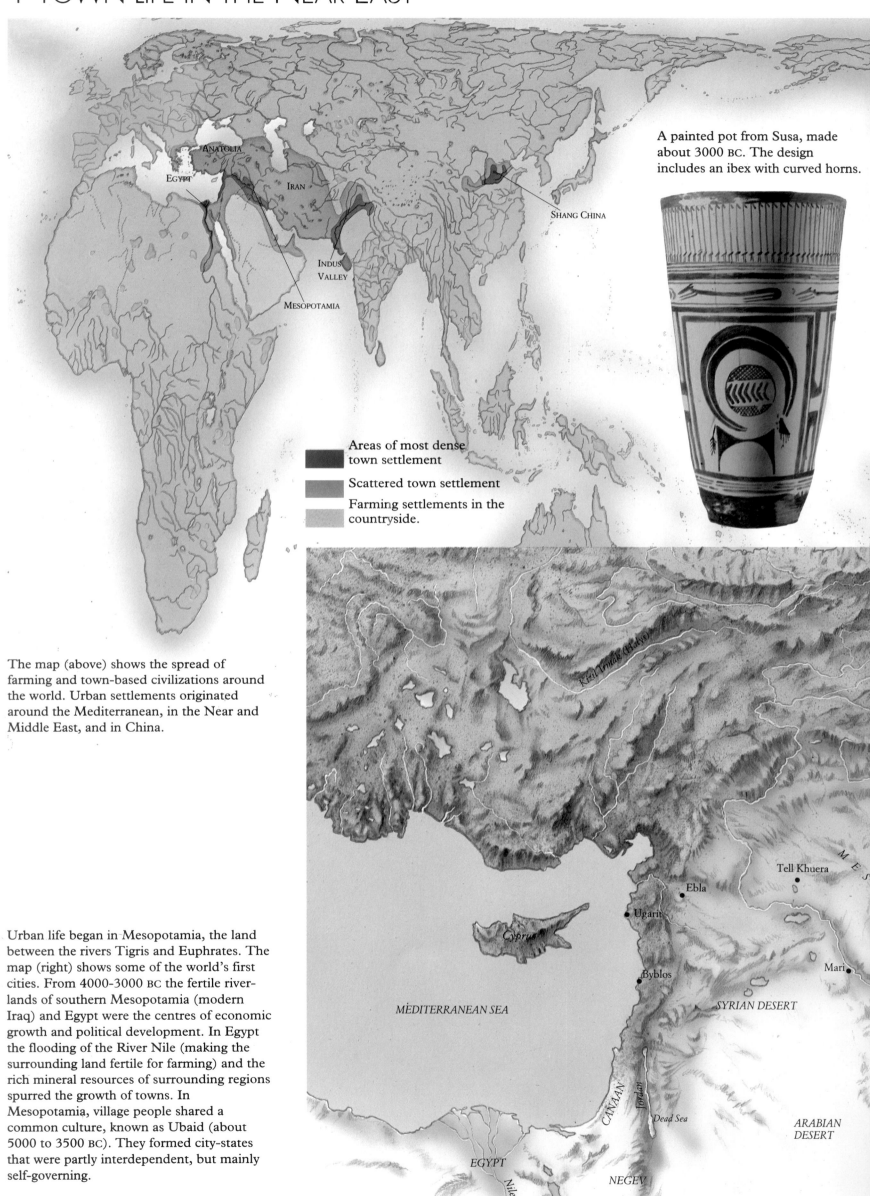

A painted pot from Susa, made about 3000 BC. The design includes an ibex with curved horns.

Areas of most dense town settlement

Scattered town settlement

Farming settlements in the countryside.

The map (above) shows the spread of farming and town-based civilizations around the world. Urban settlements originated around the Mediterranean, in the Near and Middle East, and in China.

Urban life began in Mesopotamia, the land between the rivers Tigris and Euphrates. The map (right) shows some of the world's first cities. From 4000-3000 BC the fertile river-lands of southern Mesopotamia (modern Iraq) and Egypt were the centres of economic growth and political development. In Egypt the flooding of the River Nile (making the surrounding land fertile for farming) and the rich mineral resources of surrounding regions spurred the growth of towns. In Mesopotamia, village people shared a common culture, known as Ubaid (about 5000 to 3500 BC). They formed city-states that were partly interdependent, but mainly self-governing.

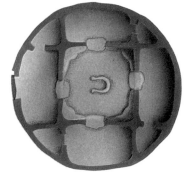

A small terracotta model of a house, from Mari. The round, walled shape (for defence) developed from the warlike traditions of northern Mesopotamia, which was less civilized than the south.

The origins of Sumer are unknown. There is no trace of earlier Stone Age people living in the region where the Sumerians founded their cities. They may have come from the north, from either the Zagros Mountains or the Caucasus. The gods of their myths were mountain-dwellers. Or they may have come from India, for there are similarities between Sumerian culture and the civilization of the Indus Valley.

There are also links, through Sumerian gods, with Bahrain, in the Gulf.

Origins of Sumer 5000 BC

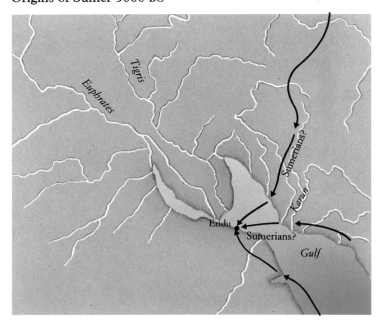

Early sites of Sumer 4000-3000 BC

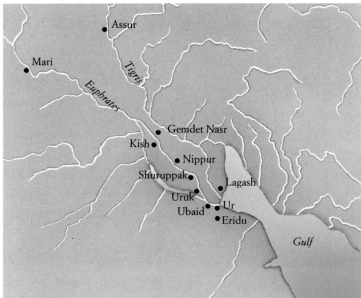

Growth of Sumer by 2000 BC

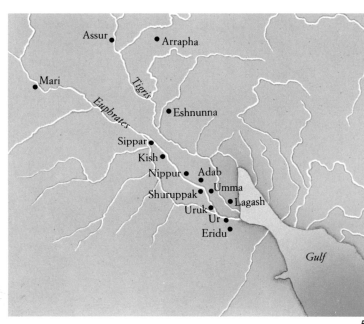

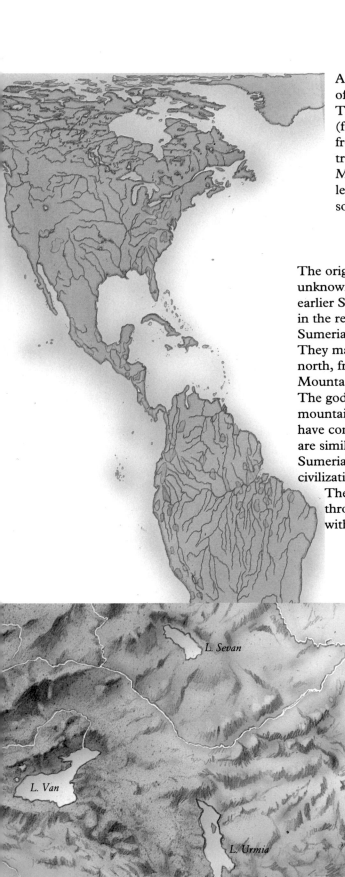

1 Town Life in the Near East

People began creating towns from about 4000 BC along the great rivers of Mesopotamia (the land between the rivers). Later this region became known as Sumer – the first civilization of the Near East. The towns grew from older farm settlements that had grown up on the hilly spurs of the mountains surrounding Mesopotamia. As populations grew, people moved into drier lands. They invented ways to irrigate the fields to secure their harvests, even when the rains failed.

Cities with brick walls

The first evidence of town-living comes from Chalcolithic times, when copper was first used, from about 6000 BC. The site of Tell el-Ubaid (Iraq) has given its name to the culture known as Ubaid, which is noted for its painted pottery decorated with geometric and sometimes animal designs.

The first settlers of southern Mesopotamia had lived in simple huts. Many people continued to do so, but the town-dwellers of Sumer built impressive public buildings and temples, using sun-dried bricks. The oldest of the Sumerian cities was (according to the Sumerians themselves) Eridu, a site excavated in the 1940s. The people living between the rivers Tigris and Euphrates established links with the east (in what is now Iran). They developed improved irrigation methods, using ditches and canals to control the rivers. The Ubaid period lasted until about 3500 BC in the south. An important site was Tepe Gawra (in what became Assyria). In the north, people were slower to build towns, but did so at Gemdet Nasr and other places such as Eshnunna. Northern towns were copied from those of the south.

A huge communal house (left), made of reeds, and similar to those still used by the Marsh Arabs of southern Iraq. Pictures of buildings like this appear on cylindrical seals and stone reliefs in Mesopotamia during the Uruk period.

The real 'explosion' of town life, with the change from a network of farming villages to a culture of flourishing towns, came next, in what is known as the Uruk period.

Temple builders of Uruk

The city of Uruk (Erech) had brick walls to keep out enemies. Its chief glory was a great artificial mound, or ziggurat, crowned by the White Temple. The temple was built shortly before 3000 BC on the remains of older sacred buildings. The walls and columns were decorated with clay tiles, in geometric patterns. It was probably dedicated to a god called Anu.

The people of the Sumerian cities were skilled craftworkers as well as builders. They made objects of gold, silver and copper.

Other city-states

Other city-states in Mesopotamia were Elam (Susa), Akkad

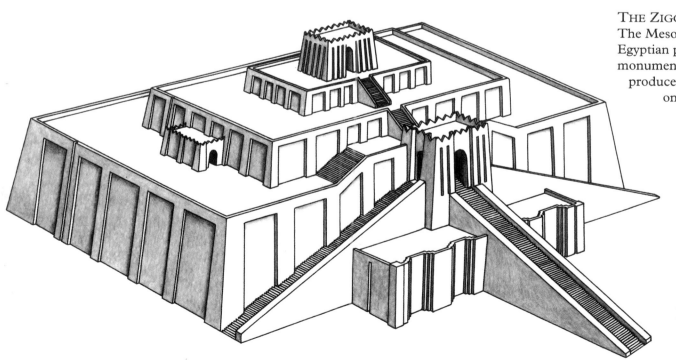

The Ziggurat

The Mesopotamian ziggurat, like the Egyptian pyramid, is the most typical monument of the civilization that produced it. Raised on platforms, one above the other, it was an artificial mountain – a pedestal to the temple of the god. The ziggurat complex was usually entered by a long stairway or by a spiral ramp – down which the gods descended during religious ceremonies. Ziggurats resemble the step pyramids of Egypt, but were not built as burial places. Its shape and the temple on top make the ziggurat more like the pyramids of ancient Central America.

Pottery (left) was decorated with geometric patterns and with stylized pictures of people and animals.

This Ubaid house (below) was split into small rooms. It has two wings, with a central courtyard, and a flat roof reached by a staircase.

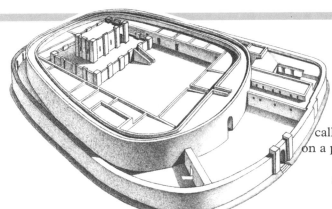

This early temple (left) at Khafajeh (Tutub) on the Diyala river was enclosed by a solid wall. It was dedicated to a god called Sin, whose shrine was on a platform in the innermost part of the temple. The attendant priest lived in a corner of the courtyard.

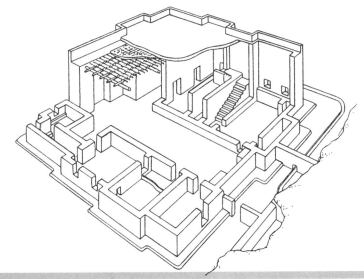

and Mari. Mari was an important stopping place for travellers on their way north to Syria, Canaan and Anatolia, and west to Egypt. Here archaeologists have found ancient writings that record the merchants' trade links with neighbouring regions.

Assur on the upper Tigris also became the centre of a strong state, based on trade. Another northern city-state, with strong links to Sumer, was Tell Khuera. Town-life spread west into Syria as Sumerian civilization began to decline. Here the most important city-state was Ebla, which also had close links with the great cities of Mesopotamia.

The civilization of the Nile

At about the same time as the Ubaid culture was flourishing in Mesopotamia, the people of Egypt were beginning to develop a civilization based on farming and irrigation. Experts can trace the development of cultures around El-Amra near Abydos and at Gerzah in the southern Fayum region. At about the same time as the Uruk temple-builders were at work, the first towns were being built in the Nile valley.

There was much contact between the two peoples, and the Egyptians were keen to follow Sumer's example. They adopted Sumerian ideas of writing, brick-making and architecture, and developed them into original Egyptian forms of enormous vitality. Egyptian civilization, and Egyptian cities, began to develop in a unique style.

Mesopotamia's influence

Mesopotamia also influenced life in Anatolia, to the north (a valuable source of copper, zinc, gold and silver). Here and further west, in Canaan, people also began building towns.

Towns were also founded on the Mediterranean coast, at Byblos and Ugarit. Towns were obvious strongpoints, and Byblos soon came so much under Egyptian influence that it was held as an Egyptian colony. Such a strong walled city had great military importance, as a fortress on the coast of a sea where Egyptian ships were now trading.

THE ORIGINS OF WRITING

People began to write during the early 3000s BC in order to record and count goods and stores. The oldest known writings are picture-signs made on clay tablets. They were made in Uruk about 3300 BC, but since the people already used a system with 700 signs, there must have been earlier writing – as yet unknown to us.

In another system, pieces of fired clay, or counters, were used as tokens to denote the type or quantity of goods. The tokens (similar in shape to the goods being traded) were sealed up into clay containers, known as *bullae* (Latin for studs). The outside of the container was stamped with marks that looked like the tokens inside.

True writing was a combination of picture-signs (pictograms) and marks like those on the *bullae*. The Sumerians wrote with pointers on wet clay tablets, making wedge-shaped marks which give their writing its name – cuneiform (wedge-shaped).

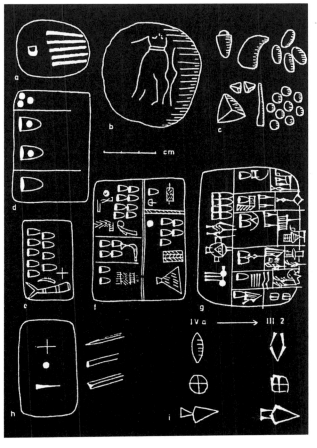

How writing evolved:
a. tablet with number signs
b. a bulla
c. counters
d. tablet with number signs
e–g. written records, from Uruk and Gemdet Nasr
h. writing 'pens' and the marks they made
i. evolution of signs, as shown by finds at Uruk.

Uruk c.3100 BC	Gemdet Nasr c.3000 BC	Protodyn. c.2400 BC	Ur III c.2000 BC	Meaning
				head
				bread
				eat
				cow
				plough
				place
•	•	•		6
				1

Examples of the development of writing in Mesopotamia.

A bronze head of a king of
Akkad, from Nineveh, around
3500-3000 BC. It is often
identified as Sargon I, but is
more probably his nephew
Naram-Sin.

The two most powerful city-states of Sumer were Ur and Lagash.
Like the other states, they were ruled by soldier-kings, who
increased their power by wars of conquest. This map shows the
conquests of Lugalzaggisi (in red) and of Sargon I (in blue).
Lugalzaggisi founded the first of the Mesopotamian empires. He
made Uruk his capital, and conquered lands stretching from the
'Inferior Sea' (the Gulf) to the 'Superior Sea' (the Mediterranean).
He fought the strong state of Ebla (in Syria), probably succeeding
only in making its rulers pay tribute. Ebla was still independent
and thriving when Lugalzaggisi was himself defeated by Sargon
of Akkad.

The spread of Ubaid civilization. In
5400 BC the Halaf culture that had dominated
northern Mesopotamia was replaced by the
more advanced Ubaid, a culture that had arisen
in the south. The Ubaid peoples were the first in
the world to have organized institutions. Their social
and administrative systems spread across the Near East,
from Iran in the east to the Mediterranean in the west. The
map shows important cities that flourished at this time.

This little silver model of a boat from Mesopotamia dates from the 3000s BC. On the map is the gold helmet of Meskalamdug, from Ur.

The map (below) shows the empire of Ur, about 2050 to 1955 BC. At the heart of the empire (dark green) were the 23 city-states of Sumer and Akkad. North and east of them (light green) were settlements ruled by military governors, collecting annual taxes. Other states (red) were allied to Ur by treaty or by marriage contracts. The inset plan shows how the temple area at Ur developed.

c.2000 BC

Temple of Nanna
Ziggurat
Palace of Ur-Nammu

1000s BC

Palace
Ziggurat
Temple of Nanna
Priests' Palace

TEMPLE AREA AT UR

L. Van
SUBARTU
Tigris
Tell el-Hawa   Bassetki
hubat-Enlil   Dur-Sharrukin
Apku
Nineveh
Qatara (Tell el-Rimah)   Arbil
Kar-Tukulti-Ninurta
Assur   Arrapha
L. Urmia
IRANIAN PLATEAU
Simurrum
Sar-e Pol-e Zohab
ZAGROS
Euphrates
Eshnunna   Der   Urua
Dur-Kurigalzu   Khafajeh
Sippar   Akshak
Akkad   Babylon
Possible site of Akkad   Kish   To Meluhha (Indus)
AKKAD   Zahara
Borsippa   Nippur
Adab   Umma   Susa
Shuruppak   Deh-e No
SUMER   Hammam
Uruk   Lagash
Ur   Al-Untash-Napirisha
Eridu   (Choga Zanbil)
ELAM
INFERIOR SEA
Gulf

Urkish   Hasanlu
Nineveh
Arbil
Assur   Arrapha
Mari   Diyala   Alman
Ishim-Shulgi
Euphrates   Eshnunna
Sippar   Urum   Der
Kazallu   Kutha   Nippur   Susa
Puzrish-Dagan   Adab   Dabrum
Isin   Girsu
Shuruppak   Uruk   Lagash
Ur   Anzan
original coastline

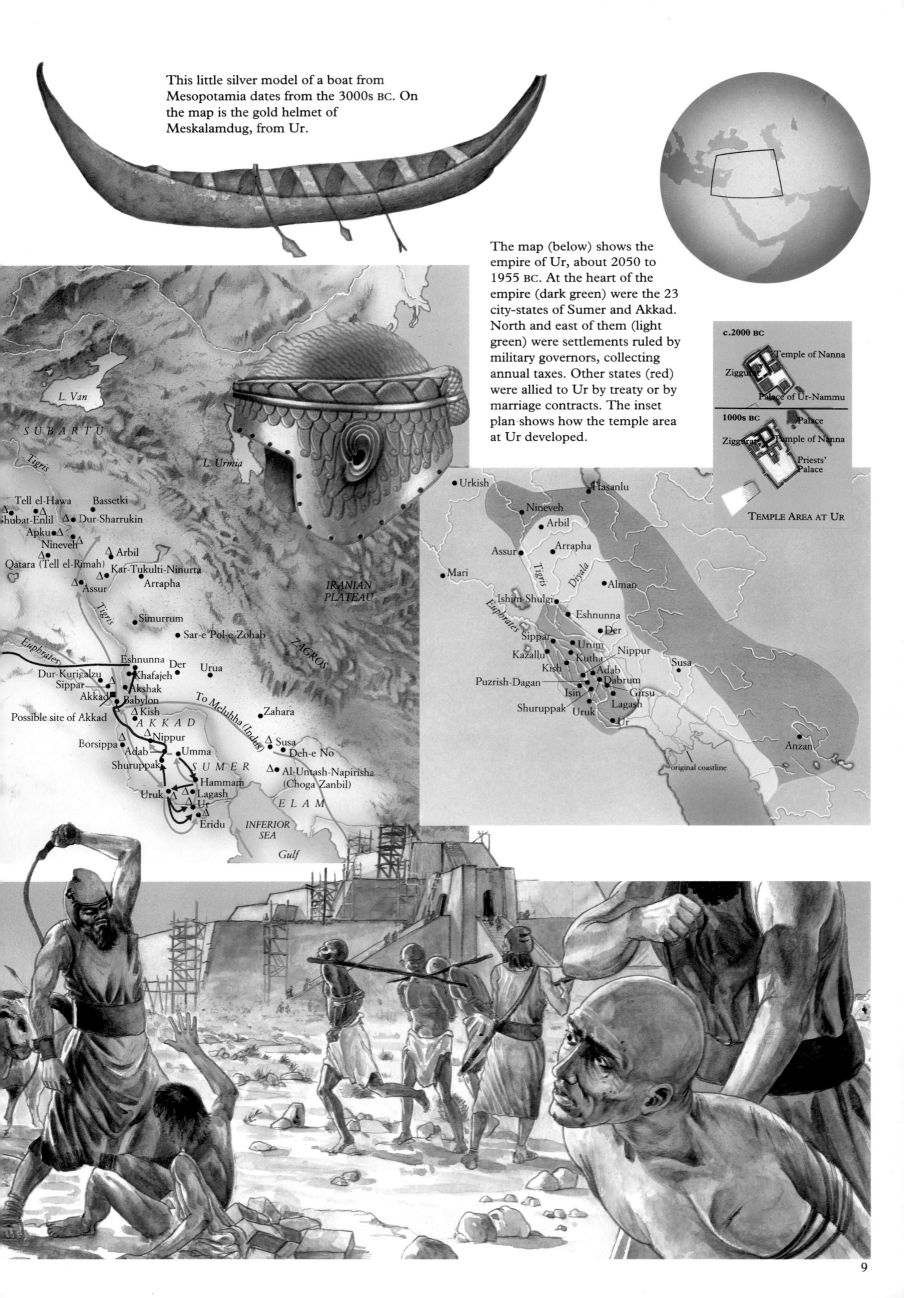

9

2 MESOPOTAMIA: CIVILIZATION AND THE CITY

By 3000 BC the urban revolution in Sumer – the growth of cities – was flourishing. With it came a new and complex process of social, economic and cultural development. The land was fertile – people grew dates, wheat and barley, and reared cattle and sheep. For minerals (gold, silver, lead, copper) they depended on trade by land, river and sea. Such an economic system needed organization, and with this came a community with clearly marked social rankings.

Village self-sufficiency
The villagers of the countryside could produce enough food to feed themselves in a normal year. Irrigation guaranteed crops, even in a dry season, and there was usually a surplus of food available for storage in warehouses and for redistribution – and sale.

Having surpluses to sell meant that people could trade with their neighbours. Within the community, those with the greatest wealth occupied the highest rank in the social hierarchy.

Workers and managers
In Sumer people specialized in different tasks. The city was the natural environment for a host of trades and crafts. At first, craftworkers, traders, officials and others not engaged in the main work of farming were paid by the farmers for their services.

As urban life developed, officials (in effect, managers and civil servants) came to be more important than humble workers, and the city became the centre for bureaucracy and government. Large public buildings were built. Officials regulated trade with neighbouring states, and maintained an army. The army was made up partly of paid soldiers (mercenaries) but mostly of young men from the farm villages who, when not at war, were employed as labour for public works such as digging irrigation canals and building roads.

Temples, kings and taxes
Sumerian cities had patron gods. The god of Ur, for example, was the moon god Nanna. The god, not the king, owned the city, but the king was still a most important personage. He was called either *en* (lord) or *lugal* (great man). He had a palace, but the god had a temple on the top of a great monumental mound called a ziggurat.

Religion was very important to the Sumerians. Each city had its own god or goddess, and there were hundreds of deities. The priests looked after the temples, aided by large numbers of helpers and slaves. Farmers gave some of their produce to the temple, either as a gift to the god, or as payment to the priests for their services. In Sumer the priests were the most dedicated tax-collectors. That is another reason why the Sumerians led the way in developing forms of writing and arithmetic.

In this scene (pictured in colour on pages 8/9) labourers are building a ziggurat, shown on the right. It is a series of platforms, one above the other, on a rectangular base. On top will be the god's house. The pyramid-like structure will be from 50 to 90 metres (160 to 300 ft) high, with three stairways.

The priest-king will lead the religious ceremonies held at the ziggurat, calling on the gods to descend from the heavens to their people below.

The shortage of building stone in Mesopotamia means that bricks are being used. These are made by the labourers, who mix clay with straw that has been soaked in water for some days. A labourer on the left is using a wooden mould to shape the wet clay bricks, which are then left to dry and harden in the hot sun for several weeks.

The labourers are almost all prisoners, captured in war. They are guarded by soldiers and driven by overseers with whips. Some are bound and yoked together by poles. The hot sun beats down, and the work is brutally hard, for there are no machines (other than ox-drawn carts). There is little relief or hope for the unfortunate captives condemned to build the monumental stone mountain.

These Sumerian signs (left) have so far not been deciphered. They are written on a terracotta tablet, found at Kish and dating from about 3000 BC.

A statuette of the Sumerian scribe Dudu (right), who came from Lagash. This man was a teacher, as well as being skilled in letters.

Sargon's fame was immortalized in Babylonian chronicles: 'Sargon, king of Akkad...had no rivals. He imposed his spell of terror over all lands'.

This remarkable ruler founded a city, Agade, which has never been excavated because its whereabouts are unknown. After Sargon's short-lived dynasty was destroyed, so too was his city. Sargon apparently rose from humble origins. He was a Semite, and served the ruler of Kish, in northern Sumer. By defeating Lugalzaggisi of Uruk, Sargon made himself lord of all southern Mesopotamia. He fought many battles to secure his victory over the city-states, and then turned his attention further afield: to Syria and Anatolia, and Susa, the capital of the Elamites in the Zagros Mountains. He encouraged trade with the Indus Valley cities, with the Gulf, Lebanon, Crete and possibly even Greece.

Sargon set up a government answerable directly to himself and managed to keep control over all the lands subject to his command. No written records made in Sargon's lifetime have been found. His deeds are known only from later accounts that mix fact with legend. According to these accounts, Sargon's latter years were troubled by rebellions.

Warring cities

Although the Sumerian cities were culturally similar, they were politically independent. Some grew very large. In three centuries, Uruk swelled from an area of 70 hectares (173 acres) in 3100 BC to 550 hectares (1,359 acres) by 2900 BC. The population reached more than 20,000. Cities like Uruk strove to control trade routes along which merchants sent goods such as metals, timber and building stone. Control of trade assured real power.

During what historians call the early dynastic period in Sumer, the cities of southern Mesopotamia fought one another. The rival Sumerians and Akkadians were actually alike, using a similar language and style of writing. But, being so close, they often quarrelled over territory. No single power succeeded in gaining complete dominance over the rest until 2334 BC, when the great king Sargon of Kish managed to gain control over the whole area and made Akkad (Agade) his capital.

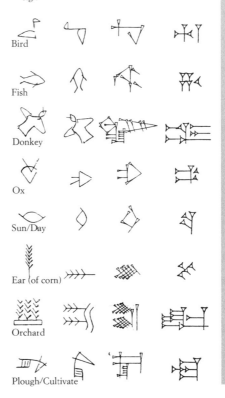

Primitive picture-sign — Cuneiform — Babylonian — Assyrian

Bird
Fish
Donkey
Ox
Sun/Day
Ear (of corn)
Orchard
Plough/Cultivate

Empires of Akkad and Ur

For the next 200 years Sargon's successors ruled his domains, the most famous of them being his nephew Naram-Sin (2254-2219 BC). Their forces moved northwest towards the Mediterranean and southeast towards the Gulf, which became the focus for a busy water-borne trade between Mesopotamia and the cities of the Indus Valley (in modern Pakistan).

For a time Mesopotamia then came under the rule of the Gutians, a somewhat uncivilized people from the Zagros Mountains. A second Sumerian Empire arose under the control of the city of Ur. This again united the whole of Sumer, but was conquered by Elam in 2000 BC.

Examples of cuneiform writing (above) show how symbols were derived from picture-signs, turned sideways, and later developed. The Sumerians used some 600 signs – they never invented a more concise, sound-based alphabet.

This small gypsum model of two people (right) was found beneath a temple floor in Nippur. The figures have eyes of lapis lazuli stuck in place with bitumen.

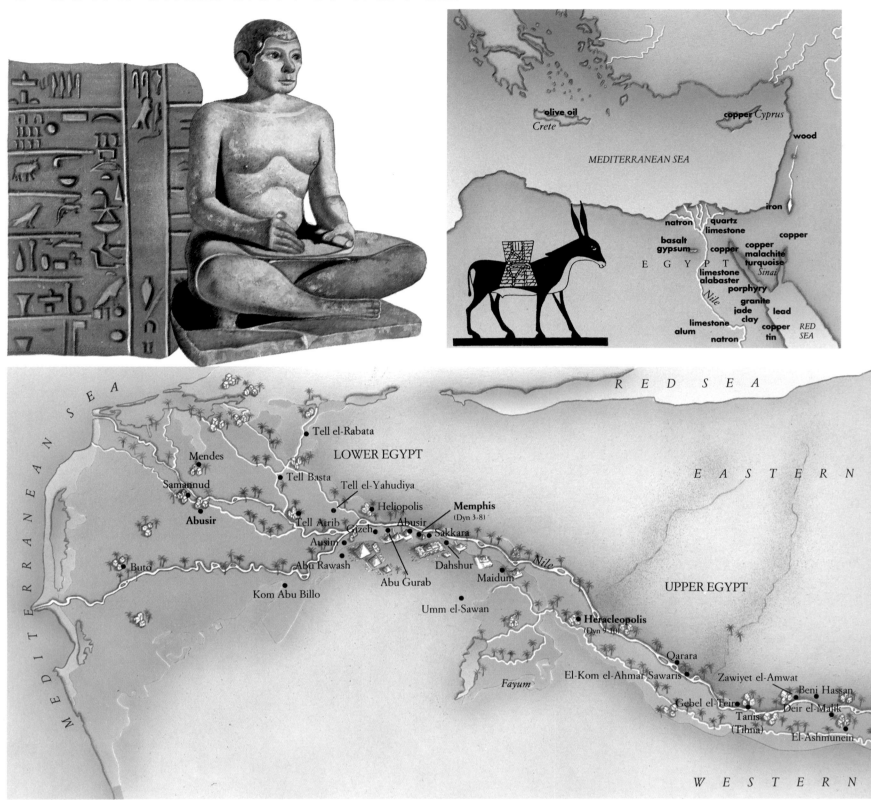

LOWER EGYPT

Tell el-Rabata
Mendes
Tell Basta
Samannud
Tell el-Yahudiya
Abusir
Heliopolis
Memphis
(Dyn 3–8)
Tell Atrib
Abusir
Gizeh
Sakkara
Ausim
Buto
Dahshur
Abu Rawash
Nile
Abu Gurab
Maidum
Kom Abu Billo
UPPER EGYPT
Umm el-Sawan
Heracleopolis
(Dyn 9–10)
Qarara
Fayum
El-Kom el-Ahmar Sawaris
Zawiyet el-Amwat
Beni Hassan
Gebel el-Teir
Deir el-Malik
Tanis
(Tihna)
El-Ashmunein

MEDITERRANEAN SEA
RED SEA
EASTERN
WESTERN

MEDITERRANEAN SEA
olive oil
Crete
copper Cyprus
wood
iron
EGYPT
natron
quartz
limestone
basalt
gypsum
copper
copper
malachite
turquoise
Sinai
limestone
alabaster
porphyry
granite
jade
clay
lead
limestone
alum
natron
copper
tin
RED
SEA
Nile

This inscription (far left) was made at Elephantine, a town in Upper Egypt (about 1450 BC). It lists offerings made each year to the gods. The writing is in Egyptian hieroglyphs, or picture symbols. Beside the inscription is a limestone figure of a scribe. This is much older, dating from between 2600 and 2500 BC. The map (left) shows how Egypt imported raw materials and other goods from a wide region.

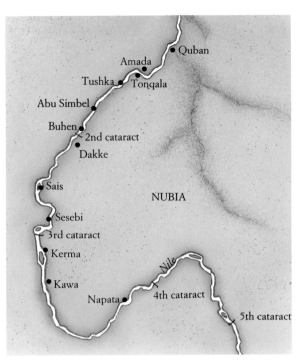

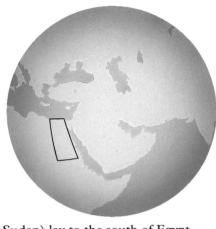

Nubia (modern Sudan) lay to the south of Egypt. Known as Kush, it was an important meeting point of cultures and peoples from Central and Saharan Africa, the Nile Valley and lands to the south, such as Ethiopia. The Nile flows through Nubia. Five of its six cataracts (rapids) are shown on the map (left), as well as important settlements in Nubia, which was finally conquered by King Thutmose I.

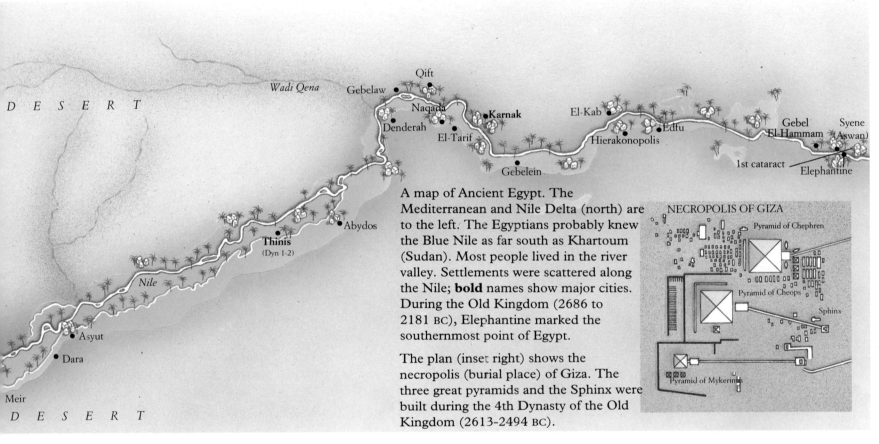

A map of Ancient Egypt. The Mediterranean and Nile Delta (north) are to the left. The Egyptians probably knew the Blue Nile as far south as Khartoum (Sudan). Most people lived in the river valley. Settlements were scattered along the Nile; **bold** names show major cities. During the Old Kingdom (2686 to 2181 BC), Elephantine marked the southernmost point of Egypt.

The plan (inset right) shows the necropolis (burial place) of Giza. The three great pyramids and the Sphinx were built during the 4th Dynasty of the Old Kingdom (2613-2494 BC).

3 EGYPT: CIVILIZATION OF THE NILE

The 'Narmer Stone' (right) comes from the 1st Dynasty. The hieroglyphic writing on it is a mixture of picture-signs and sound-signs, and the text recounts a key moment in Egypt's history – the uniting of the two kingdoms.

North Africa became drier and less habitable in the 4000s BC. This climatic change encouraged people to settle beside the great River Nile. The river flooded every year and the mud carried down by its floodwaters gave the Nile its Egyptian name 'Ar', or 'Black'. Along the banks of the river people could grow the crops essential to life, and they could also use the river for transport.

Groups of people formed communities, working together to irrigate the land and build dykes to protect their homes from the Nile floods. Each year the river washed down huge amounts of silt from its mountain sources; this silt made the land fertile.

The first kingdoms

Villages came under the control of two kingdoms. One ruled Lower Egypt, the land around the Nile Delta (the north). The other controlled Upper Egypt (the south). In about 3100 BC, a king called Menes (also known as Narmer) from Upper Egypt overcame Lower Egypt.

Egypt was now one kingdom, and Menes built a capital for himself at Memphis on the border between Upper and Lower Egypt, not far from modern Cairo. His was the first of 20 dynasties that governed Egypt until the time of Alexander the Great (322 BC).

Tombs of the mighty

The early rulers of Egypt were buried in the sacred city of Abydos, while their most important officials were laid to rest inside crude brick tombs at Sakkara. A king called Zoser (2630-2611 BC) decided he wanted to be buried at Sakkara, but not in an ordinary tomb. His tomb was to be a huge step pyramid, rising heavenwards, so that he could

This amulet (right) is a charm made of terracotta. It shows the sacred eye of the god Horus.

ascend to the gods. The kings of Egypt were now so powerful that they thought themselves divine.

With Zoser, Egypt entered a new period, known as the Old Kingdom. This was when the Great Pyramids of Giza were built. The king was identified with the sun, and it was thought his soul could reach heaven without the need for crude steps. The sheer stone sides of the pyramids were like the rays of the sun.

The three most famous pyramids are at Giza. They were built for Khufu, or Cheops (2551-2528 BC), Chephren (2520-2494 BC) and Mykerinus, or Menkere (2490-2472 BC). Truly wonders of the world, these monumental structures represented an enormous investment of time, resources and human effort.

Pyramid-building (pictured in colour on pages 12/13) called for tremendous organization and huge physical effort. The scale of the task can hardly be imagined today.

From distant quarries, huge blocks of stone, each weighing 15 tonnes (14.7 tons), were dragged to the river and loaded on to boats for shipment to the tomb site.

Hundreds of thousands of slaves moved the stones into place, their aching muscles aided only by wooden rollers and sleds dragged over plank tracks. The pace of work was kept up by watchful overseers, and directed by the king's architect. Scribes recorded details of materials, cost and time.

As the pyramid rose higher, the stones had to be heaved up ramps of compressed sand to the top. Between 200,000 and 300,000 limestone blocks were needed.

The pyramid was finally sheathed in smooth white casing stones.

The work took many years, and thousands of slaves toiled and died during the pyramid-building. The tomb of the king took precedence over everything and everyone.

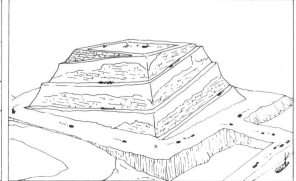

A terracotta falcon amulet (left). The falcon was the symbol of Horus, the god of the sky.

Egyptians abroad

During the Old Kingdom, Egypt was busy trading with and gaining power over its neighbours. Armies marched south into Nubia, seeking slaves and ivory. Raids from desert peoples were repulsed, and areas with valuable resources (such as Sinai, with its copper) were acquired.

In reed boats, Egyptians explored the Nile and ventured out to sea, to explore the Mediterranean coast. They went down the Red Sea to the land of Punt (modern Ethiopia and Somalia) to trade for precious woods, myrrh (used to make perfumes), gold and exotic animals.

Ruling over all

The king, or pharaoh, was a supreme ruler. In fact, the title 'pharaoh' was not used until after about 1500 BC, but the early kings wielded equally wide powers. Egypt's ruler was a god in human form and as such had unquestioned authority. The pharaoh governed through provincial officials, who were given charge of regions called nomes. Each governor was aided by priests, generals and scribes.

Not all Egypt's rulers were strong and successful. Sometimes invaders attacked, and sometimes there was civil war as local governors tried to control the nomes for their own ends. For a short time, the city of Heracleopolis was the centre of power. Then, in the 11th dynasty, a strong ruler called Mentuhotep (2061-2010 BC) united Egypt. He ruled from Thebes. Egypt stayed united, and its civilization remained impressive and practically unchanged for the next two thousand years.

THE GREAT PYRAMID
Inside the pyramid were narrow corridors leading to the burial chambers. In the Great Pyramid, the queen's chamber is the smaller, beneath the king's, but she was probably not buried there. The entrance to the tomb was well above ground level, and inside, as in most pyramids, there was a fake passage leading to a false burial chamber – to outwit tomb robbers.

Each pyramid was part of a larger complex, containing temples for the funeral ceremonies, priests' houses and warehouses. From about 2700 to 1700 BC, Egypt's kings were buried within pyramids, though none matched Khufu's in size. Treasures were entombed with them – the goods they would need in the afterlife.

Four royal crowns (left, from top to bottom): of Upper Egypt, of Lower Egypt, of the unified kingdom, and the war crown.

This wooden model (left) is of a granary from the Old Kingdom. It has high walls enclosing the grainstore, which is flat roofed, with a parapet around the top. Grain was poured in through the round hole in the top, and emptied through the square windows. Wheat and barley were the grain crops grown in Egypt.

15

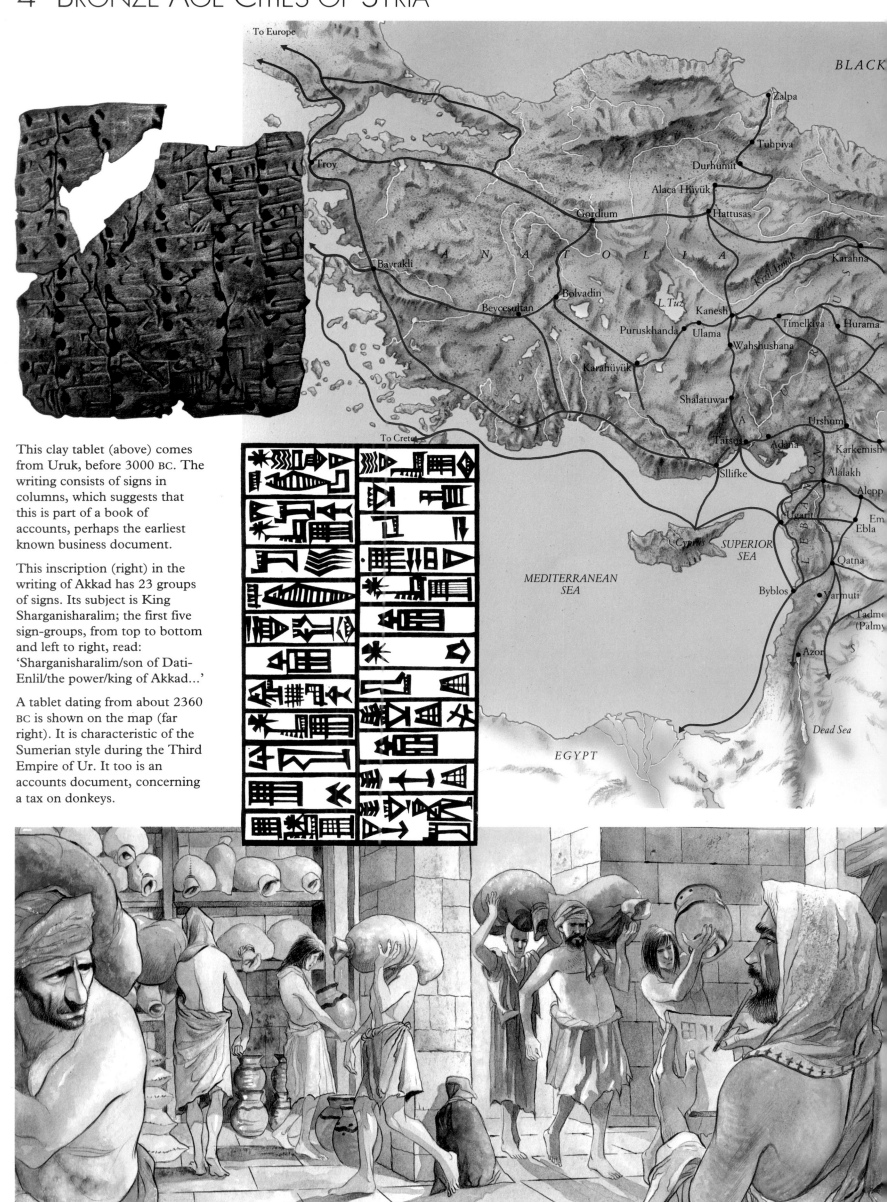

This clay tablet (above) comes from Uruk, before 3000 BC. The writing consists of signs in columns, which suggests that this is part of a book of accounts, perhaps the earliest known business document.

This inscription (right) in the writing of Akkad has 23 groups of signs. Its subject is King Sharganisharalim; the first five sign-groups, from top to bottom and left to right, read: 'Sharganisharalim/son of Dati-Enlil/the power/king of Akkad...'

A tablet dating from about 2360 BC is shown on the map (far right). It is characteristic of the Sumerian style during the Third Empire of Ur. It too is an accounts document, concerning a tax on donkeys.

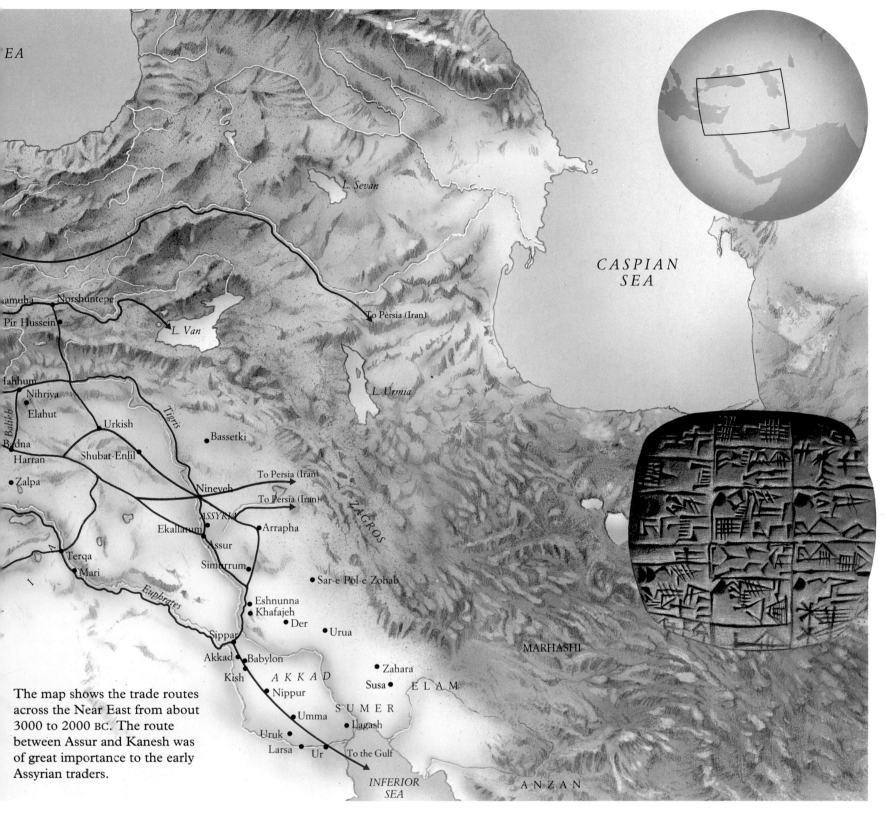

The map shows the trade routes across the Near East from about 3000 to 2000 BC. The route between Assur and Kanesh was of great importance to the early Assyrian traders.

Labels on map: EA, L. Sevan, CASPIAN SEA, amuha, Norshuntepe, Pir Hussein, L. Van, To Persia (Iran), L. Urmia, Iahhum, Nihriya, Elahut, Balikh, Bdna, Urkish, Tigris, Bassetki, Harran, Shubat-Enlil, Zalpa, Nineveh, To Persia (Iran), To Persia (Iran), ZAGROS, ASSYRIA, Ekallatum, Arrapha, Assur, Terqa, Simurrum, Mari, Euphrates, Sar-e Pol-e Zohab, Eshnunna, Khafajeh, Der, Urua, MARHASHI, Sippar, Akkad, Babylon, AKKAD, Zahara, Kish, Susa, ELAM, Nippur, SUMER, Umma, Ilagash, Uruk, Larsa, Ur, To the Gulf, INFERIOR SEA, ANZAN

4 BRONZE AGE CITIES OF SYRIA

A soldier leads a captive on this tablet (below) from Mari. The figures are inlaid with mother-of-pearl on schist (a crystalline rock).

Ancient Syria developed an urban civilization alongside those of Egypt and Mesopotamia. At the end of the third millennium BC, the power of the third Sumerian dynasty began to diminish. By this time, town culture had spread throughout much of the Near East and had moved into regions with very different environments from that of Mesopotamia.

Bronze Age kingdoms

The growth of towns was accompanied by a new development – the use of new metals. Bronze tools and weapons replaced copper ones in Sumer as early as 3500 BC.

Powerful city-states controlled the various trade routes in and out of Mesopotamia. In the northern dry lands, Assur on the river Tigris controlled the trade into Anatolia. Its merchants crossed the mountains, with donkey loads of wool and tin, to the markets of Kanesh (modern Kultepe). They returned with copper, gold and silver.

On the Euphrates, the city of Mari (modern Tall al-Hariri in Syria) guarded the trade to the east. In Syria, Ebla dominated the northern and Mediterranean routes. Karkemish on the upper Euphrates guarded trade between Syria and Anatolia, being a stopping point on the road to Kanesh.

In central Syria the independent kingdom of Qatna controlled the route to southern Syria, Galilee and the Mediterranean ports of Ugarit and Byblos.

Fortified for defence

These guard-kingdoms and cities were often at war with one another. This led to a growth in large fortified towns, and a decrease in the number of scattered (and less easily defended) villages. The ruler's palace, not the temple, was becoming the real centre of power. Records on clay tablets found at Mari, one of the most important Syrian cities, mention more than 400 town names, but only a few have been identified.

The new kingdoms' rulers, and their officials, tried to make people stay within their bounds. Wandering herdsmen were faced with new laws forbidding their nomadic lifestyle. The rulers wanted people they could call to arms when attacked (and whom they could tax easily).

Nomad invasions and empires

By about 1900 BC the most powerful rulers were trying to

The storehouses and libraries of Ebla (pictured in colour on pages 16/17) were at the heart of the city's success.

At the site of Tell Mardik in Syria, archaeologists have revealed some of the secrets of the ancient city of Ebla. They have found about 15,000 clay tablets

and fragments of writing in cuneiform letters. These are mainly to do with the law and government, but the Syrians also enjoyed literature and stories.

The palace was both the king's home and the central office for tax collection and stock-taking. People brought in produce to be

checked and counted. Scribes recorded on clay tablets details of harvests, contracts, permits, people's comings and goings, letters, royal decrees and ritual procedures. The finished tablets were hardened in ovens, then stored carefully away like books on library shelves.

Around 1600 BC, Ebla was sacked and the palace was burned, probably by the Hittites. The wooden library shelves became ashes, but the clay tablets survived and were found intact more than 3500 years later.

This bronze tablet (left) from Byblos was inscribed between 2000 and 1500 BC. The inscription reads from right to left (not left to right as in English).

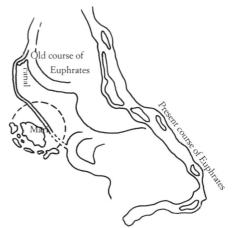

An ivory head (right), found in a palace at Ebla, from about 1700 BC. The headdress is similar to that worn by the Egyptian god Osiris.

weld other states into larger federations under their control. Shamshi-Adad (who lived in the 1700s BC) was an Amorite king from the mid-Euphrates area. The Amorites were a nomadic people from either Syria or Arabia, who began moving into Mesopotamia and Syria in the 2000s BC and setting up their own kingdoms. Shamshi-Adad created an empire out of nothing, conquering Assur and making his capital at Shubat-Enlil, in northern Assyria. He ruled a domain that stretched from Lebanon to the Zagros Mountains, and his sons held the kingdoms of Mari and Ekallatum, protecting his western and eastern boundaries. His empire was short-lived. It ended in 1757 BC when the great king died.

Another Amorite king, Rim-Sim of Larsa, was no more successful. He came up against the powerful Hammurabi of Babylon (see pages 22-23) – who was himself of Amorite origins.

The map (left) shows the site of Mari, one of the great Syrian cities. It was linked by canals to the Euphrates river, whose course has altered over the centuries.

A reconstruction of the 'Palm court' in the royal palace of Mari (below). This palace replaced an earlier one which had been destroyed, and was enormous – evidence of the Syrian kings' wealth.

The Mediterranean coast

The cities of the east, in Lebanon and Palestine, were slower to grow at first, but developed into important centres for trade and commerce. Most of what is known about the coastal region comes from Egyptian records, listing the names of Egypt's foes (these were written on clay jars and statues which were then ritually smashed, to show Egypt's contempt for all rivals). Despite this, Egypt normally traded peacefully with its northern (and weaker) neighbours.

There were walled cities at Byblos, Jericho and Megiddo, and at Jerusalem (first mentioned in about 1900 BC). These cities survived upheaval and war, and prospered. Other smaller cities disappeared, probably during the Amorite invasions, which brought a break in the progress of civilization in Syria and Palestine.

5 STRUGGLE FOR POWER IN MESOPOTAMIA

The main map shows how Mesopotamia was threatened by war from the Amorites (red arrow) and from Elam (green arrow) to the east. This twin threat persuaded the king of Babylon to extend his realm across all of Mesopotamia.

The small map (below) shows the empire of Hammurabi, from 1792 BC to its peak about 1750 BC. The arrows show the Babylonian king's campaigns against Larsa and Elam (south and east) and against Mari and Assyria (west and north).

BLACK SEA

Shamuha

Norshuntepe

URARTU

L. Sevan

CASPIAN SEA

L. Van

Iahhum

Nihriya

Elahut

Urkish

Shubat-Enlil

L. Urmia

Badna

Harran

Za·pa

Emar

Tuttul

Nineveh

ASSYRIA

ZAGROS

SYRIA

Assur

Tigris

Arrapha

Euphrates

Mari

SHIMASHKI

Tadmor (Palmyra)

Eshnunna

Amorite wall

Sippar

Babylon

Nippur

ELAM

Susa

Isin

Uruk

Larsa

Ur

Anzan

Eridu

The Code of Hammurabi was written on a stone slab, or stele, and set up in a temple. It contains 282 articles, and is the largest (though not the earliest) collection of laws from the ancient Near East. Hammurabi claimed his laws were dictated to him by the Sun-god Shamash. Part of the stele (below) shows the king and the seated god.

5 STRUGGLE FOR POWER IN MESOPOTAMIA

After the empires of Lugalzaggisi and Sargon (see pages 8/11), the peoples of Sumer and Akkad had to fight off first the Gutians, and then further invasions from the Elamites in the east and the Amorites in the north. The Amorites spoke a Semitic language, and the language of Sumer was relegated to the far south, although it was still used by priests and scholars.

Cities change hands

Cities such as Susa and Ur passed from one power to another; first held by Akkad, then by Elam, then by Sumer. In 2004 BC the ruler of the Elamite territory of Anzan, Kindattu, sacked Ur and took its king captive. Within ten years, the king of Isin, Ishbi-Ezzar, had driven the Elamites out of Ur, and founded his own dynasty there. The Isin dynasty was then overthrown by Larsa. It was a period of power struggles between warrior kings. Susa finally broke away from Mesopotamia and became part of the Elamite empire.

Despite these conflicts, the Mesopotamian peoples continued to trade across the Gulf, as far as Bahrain, Oman and the Indus Valley.

Hammurabi of Babylon

In the 1700s BC a new empire arose. It did not last long but it transformed Mesopotamia. It was created by Hammurabi, king of Babylon. He too was of Amorite origin. In less than twenty years he conquered Uruk and Isin, and defeated Larsa (with the help of the people of Mari whom he then added to his conquests).

Hammurabi used water as a weapon: damming rivers to cause floods or to force his enemies into submission by denying them water.

This decoration from a tomb of one of the kings of Ur seems to show a battle between a mythological hero and two human-headed bulls.

A maker of laws

Hammurabi is remembered for his 'code', or collection, of laws. It was modelled on existing laws, but it was the largest law code assembled. Its 282 provisions dealt with many aspects of life including family rights, trade, slavery, tariffs and taxes, prices and wages. The laws tell us much about Babylonian society.

The king was the high priest of the supreme god. So he was a religious as well as secular ruler. Beneath him were three lower classes of people: freemen, people dependent on the state, and slaves. The royal palace was now the most important place in the kingdom, not the temple. Private businesses developed, for trade was no longer centrally controlled. Contracts, loans and transfers of ownership (of

A night-time view of Babylon (pictured in colour on pages 20/21). From the summit of the great ziggurat overlooking the

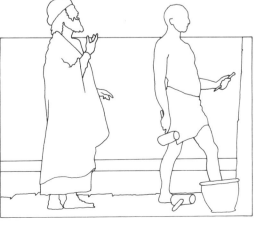

city, priests are studying the stars to read the future. They believed that the movements of the stars and the planets foretold events on earth. The Babylonians were expert mathematicians and astronomers. They divided the year into 360 days, each of 24 hours.

Hammurabi was a powerful ruler, yet he did not seek to be made a god in his lifetime – like other kings of the ancient world. He ordered his laws to be 'known by all at all times', including the command (not often followed by rulers) that 'the strong should not injure the weak'.

A symbolic picture of the universe is painted on this ceramic plate (left) from Elam.

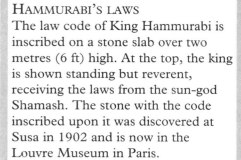

An onager, or wild ass, on a reins' ring (above) belonging to a queen of Ur.

HAMMURABI'S LAWS

The law code of King Hammurabi is inscribed on a stone slab over two metres (6 ft) high. At the top, the king is shown standing but reverent, receiving the laws from the sun-god Shamash. The stone with the code inscribed upon it was discovered at Susa in 1902 and is now in the Louvre Museum in Paris.

The laws themselves help scholars understand Babylonian society. The punishments for crimes are mostly in the form of retaliation – 'an eye for an eye, a tooth for a tooth'. But there are also examples of compensation, by payment of fines. The laws are not the same for rich and poor, but the weak were afforded some protection against the tyranny of the strong.

The Code of Hammurabi was not the only law code in Mesopotamia, nor the oldest, but is the only one we have written in stone. Older laws, such as those of Ur-Nammu of Sumer, were certainly written down but are now lost. Other kings of Sumer issued decrees and orders of a similar kind, before Hammurabi's. These more ancient laws favour compensation for offences, rather than retaliation.

Hammurabi's laws and old Hebrew laws, which they in some ways resemble, probably derive from a common heritage of Near Eastern law – one of the most lasting products of early civilizations.

land, for example) were all drawn up between individual wealthy citizens.

After Hammurabi

Hammurabi's reign ended in warfare with powerful enemies combining against him. His son Samsuluna fought against the king of Larsa, who was also ruler of Nippur. Uruk and Larsa both fell to the Babylonians and the cities of southern Mesopotamia were left desolate for centuries. One possible cause is that Samsuluna diverted the waters of the Euphrates during his war with Larsa, producing ecological catastrophe in the region.

The Amorite dynasty held Babylon and the cities of the Euphrates valley up to the 1500s BC, when they were challenged by new enemies: the Hittites. These newcomers had technology on their side – they had iron swords and spears, and rode in horse-drawn chariots.

The Hittites swept across the empire and in 1595 BC Babylon itself was destroyed. Then the Hittites retreated, and Mesopotamia was taken over by yet more invaders, the Kassites from Iran. Although they never wholly became 'Babylonians', the Kassites took over the cities and government system that had served the empire so long.

A terracotta head of an Elamite ruler or priest (above), possibly from Susa. The Elamites' original main deities were goddesses, and women were important in the royal family line.

A carving (right) of a winged goddess from Sumer, perhaps Lilith, who led souls to the kingdom of the dead. Lilith's name (meaning 'Night Monster') was given to a female demon of Jewish folklore.

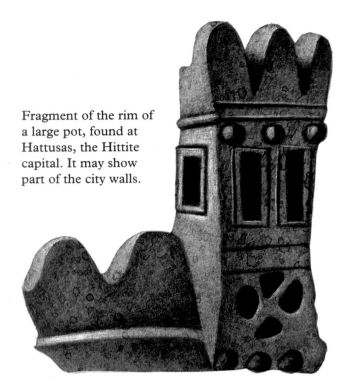

Fragment of the rim of a large pot, found at Hattusas, the Hittite capital. It may show part of the city walls.

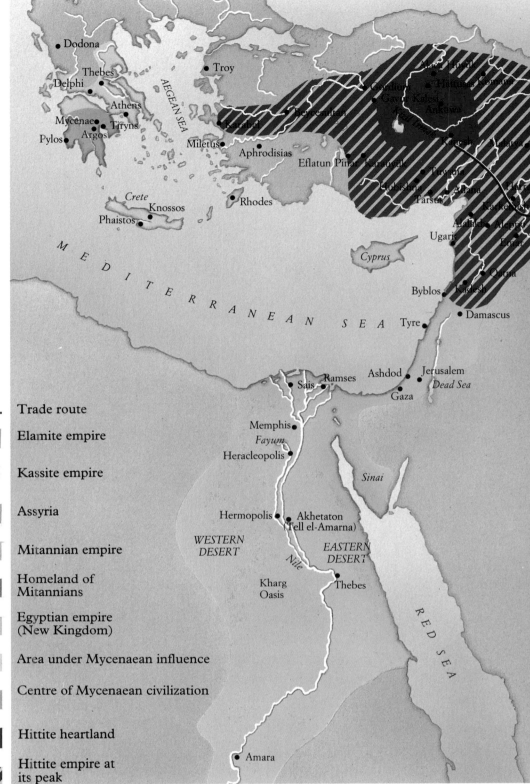

PLAN OF HATTUSAS

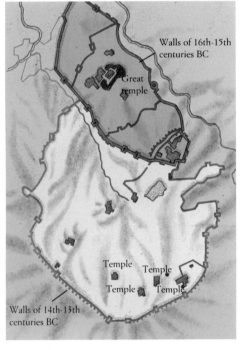

Walls of 16th-15th centuries BC

Great temple

Temple
Temple
Temple
Temple

Walls of 14th-13th centuries BC

Dodona

Thebes
Delphi
Athens
AEGEAN SEA
Troy
Mycenae
Tiryns
Pylos
Argos
Miletus
Aphrodisias
Hattusas
Ankuwa
Gordium
Eflatun Pinar
Ugarit
Kadesh
Crete
Knossos
Rhodes
Phaistos

Cyprus

MEDITERRANEAN SEA

Byblos
Tyre
Damascus

Ramses
Ashdod
Jerusalem
Sais
Dead Sea
Gaza

Memphis
Fayum
Heracleopolis

Sinai

Hermopolis
Akhetaton
(Tell el-Amarna)
WESTERN
DESERT
EASTERN
DESERT

Nile

Kharg
Oasis
Thebes

RED SEA

Amara

 Trade route

Elamite empire

Kassite empire

Assyria

Mitannian empire

Homeland of Mitannians

Egyptian empire (New Kingdom)

Area under Mycenaean influence

Centre of Mycenaean civilization

Hittite heartland

Hittite empire at its peak

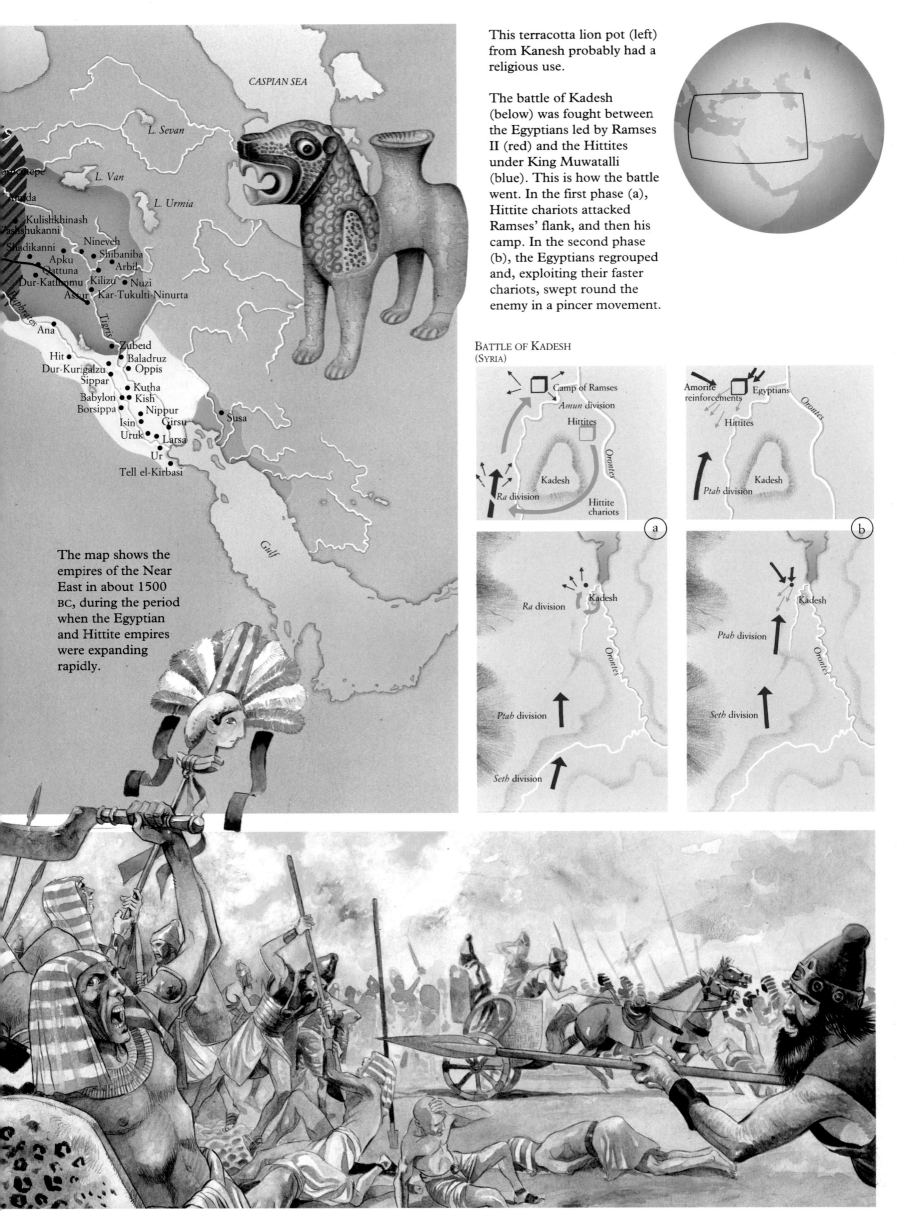

CASPIAN SEA

L. Sevan

L. Van

L. Urmia

Kulishkhinash
Tashshukanni
Shadikanni
Apku
Qattuna
Dur-Katlimmu
Assur

Nineveh
Shibaniba
Arbil
Kilizu   Nuzi
Kar-Tukulti-Ninurta

Ana

Hit
Dur-Kurigalzu
Sippar
Babylon
Borsippa

Zubeid
Baladruz
Oppis
Kutha
Kish
Nippur   Girsu
Isin
Uruk   Larsa
Ur
Tell el-Kirbasi

Susa

Gulf

The map shows the empires of the Near East in about 1500 BC, during the period when the Egyptian and Hittite empires were expanding rapidly.

This terracotta lion pot (left) from Kanesh probably had a religious use.

The battle of Kadesh (below) was fought between the Egyptians led by Ramses II (red) and the Hittites under King Muwatalli (blue). This is how the battle went. In the first phase (a), Hittite chariots attacked Ramses' flank, and then his camp. In the second phase (b), the Egyptians regrouped and, exploiting their faster chariots, swept round the enemy in a pincer movement.

BATTLE OF KADESH
(SYRIA)

Camp of Ramses
Amun division
Hittites
Kadesh
Ra division
Hittite chariots
Orontes

(a)

Amorite reinforcements
Egyptians
Hittites
Kadesh
Ptah division
Orontes

(b)

Ra division   Kadesh
Ptah division
Seth division
Orontes

Ptah division   Kadesh
Ptah division
Seth division
Orontes

6 CLASH OF EMPIRES

Early Hittite writing (right). The picture-signs are jumbled, with little sign of ordered arrangement in rows or columns.

In this later writing, the symbols stand for sounds and are arranged in a more orderly pattern.

The Hittites, who originally came from central Anatolia, founded their first empire in about 1500 BC. They built a capital at Hattusas (Bogazköy). In the reign of King Mursilis I, they sacked Babylon (1595 BC) and came to control southern Mesopotamia and also much of Syria. After a period of decline, the Hittites began to expand again to create a second empire. This New Empire reached out to engulf the Hittites' neighbours and challenge the might of Egypt.

Egypt's New Kingdom

From about 1700 BC Egypt had been fighting the Hyksos, or 'foreign rulers', whom later Greek writers called 'shepherd kings'. These Asiatic people came from the east and north. They had better weapons and horses than the Egyptians, and were able to take advantage of the weak Egyptian king and seize the throne of Egypt for themselves. But from 1554 BC the Egyptians regained the upper hand, driving out the Hyksos and creating a New Kingdom.

Under a new line of strong rulers, such as Thutmose I and his daughter Hatshepsut, Egypt's armies were victorious. In the 1400s BC, Thutmose III brought Palestine and Syria under his control. Egypt's empire was extended as far as the Euphrates in the east and into Nubia in the south. Egypt was again the great power of the Middle East. Its armies used chariots, a military skill learned from the Hyksos.

The Mitannians

Among the peoples with whom Egypt went to war were the Mitannians, who were a major power in the affairs of the Near East. They were an offshoot of the Hurrians, a northern people who had come originally from the southern Caucasus region and set up a number of smaller states. The Mitannians controlled the most powerful of these states.

Little is known about them – not even the site of their capital city Washshukann. What is known comes from Egyptian and Hittite writings. Mitannian princes probably visited the Egyptian court, along with other ambassadors from friendly or subject states. Egypt's armies fought, but did not crush, the Mitannians. Eventually, the Mitannians were conquered by the Hittites, who took over the central and western parts of their empire, while the Syrians seized the eastern part.

This scene is from the battle of Kadesh (shown in colour on pages 24/25), the first major battle in history between two properly organized armies with well-planned tactics.

Kadesh was a Hittite stronghold. Each side – Egyptians and Hittites – had about 20,000 soldiers, including infantry and cavalry mounted in chariots. The Hittites had about 2,500 chariots. Each carried three men to the Egyptians' two. The Egyptians had learned chariot warfare from fighting the Hyksos. Their soldiers used short swords and curved sickle-shaped scimitars. Both armies had spearmen, who either threw or stabbed with their weapons, and archers. The Hittites wore body armour, while the Egyptians were more lightly clad. Only the pharaoh himself wore a metal helmet.

The Egyptian divisions were scattered by the Hittite charge, leaving Ramses and his personal bodyguard in their chariots surrounded and in great danger. Ramses is shown here cutting his way through his foes in his distinctive war chariot.

Fortunately for Ramses, reinforcements arrived in time and he could claim a victory, even though his army failed to capture Kadesh.

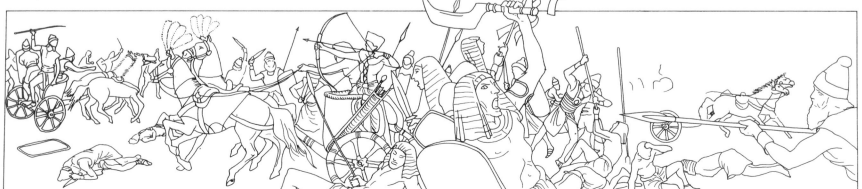

The Hittite weather god, Tarhun (left), holding a hammer (thunder) in one hand and a lightning bolt in the other. He was the chief god.

A Hittite view of the cosmos (above), carved in terracotta. The king and queen of the gods emerge from the universe-sphere.

A lion-headed demon with wings (right), from a Hittite relief found at Yazilikaya.

The winged sun (right) was the symbol of the Hittite sun cult.

Hittites and Egyptians collide

As the Hittites became more powerful, they established control over the whole of Anatolia and extended southwards into what is now Lebanon. This was normally an area of Egyptian influence, but for a time Egypt was distracted by the internal problems surrounding the religious reforms of Amenhotep IV. This king, who reigned from 1379 to 1362 BC, was an intellectual and idealist rather than a soldier and hunter like his predecessors.

It was inevitable, however, that one day Egypt and Hittite ambitions would clash. The two empires fought near the Orontes river, in Syria, at Kadesh. Kadesh was the site of an earlier Egyptian victory over the Syrians, but had come under Hittite rule about a hundred years before the battle, which was fought some time between 1299 and 1288 BC.

An armed peace

The battle at Kadesh ended in a draw, and an uneasy truce between Hittites and Egyptians. Ramses II married the Hittite king's daughter to cement the pact.

Both empires now faced rebellions within their borders and threats from outside, from the 'Sea Peoples'. The origin of these raiders is not known for certain, but they seem to have come from the west, from the Mediterranean. Among them were the Philistines.

Ramses III of Egypt fought the Sea Peoples. The Hittites fell before the invaders and by about 1200 BC their empire was no more. Since the Mitannians had also lost their empire, the Assyrians were now able to assert their power. They extended their rule into Mesopotamia as far as Nineveh. The Assyrian king Assurubalit I married his daughter to the king of Babylon, and also wrote letters to the king of Egypt. During the 1200s BC the Syrian empire became ever more powerful and flourished in succeeding centuries.

A tomb relief showing people sending sacred messages to the gods (right). The Hittites believed in a mixture of prayer and magic. The god was the master, the human the servant.

This reconstruction (right) of a gateway in the walls of Hattusas (Bogazköy), capital of the Hittite empire, shows what a formidable stronghold the city must have been.

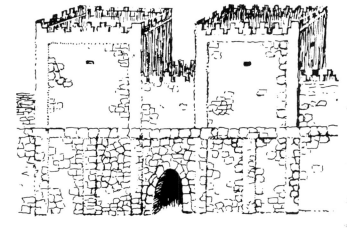

On the small map (right), the arrows show migrations of people in the second millennium BC. Crete was the centre from which culture, trade, art and ideas flowed.

The big map shows military expeditions and migrations of Achaean and Aegean peoples, fleeing from the invading Dorians and other Indo-European peoples. Cities underlined (Corinth) had Mycenaean palaces. Those in bold (**Knossos**) had Cretan palaces.

A brightly painted reconstruction shows how the great palace at Knossos must have looked.

A wall painting (far right) from Knossos shows a dancer. Below it is the 'Phaistos disc', which is marked with 45 signs. They are a form of writing, but since the disc was discovered in 1908 their meaning has baffled experts.

Map labels: INDO-EUROPEANS, Troy, Euboea, Corinth, Athens, Mycenae, Miletus, IONIAN SEA, CRETANS, Ialysos, Rhodes, Knossos, Crete

ILLYRIAN, LIBURNIANS, PHILISTINES, Corfu, Leucas, To Taranto (Tarentum), PINDUS, EPYRUS, Dodona, DORIANS, AETOLIA, L. Trichonis, Kalydon, Karditsa, Metropolis, Achelous, Ithaca, Kephallenia, Dyme, ELIS, ACH, Zakynthos, Olympia, IONIAN SEA, Kakovatos, MESSEN, Malth, Pylos, Rou, Koryphasion, ACHAEANS, To Syracuse

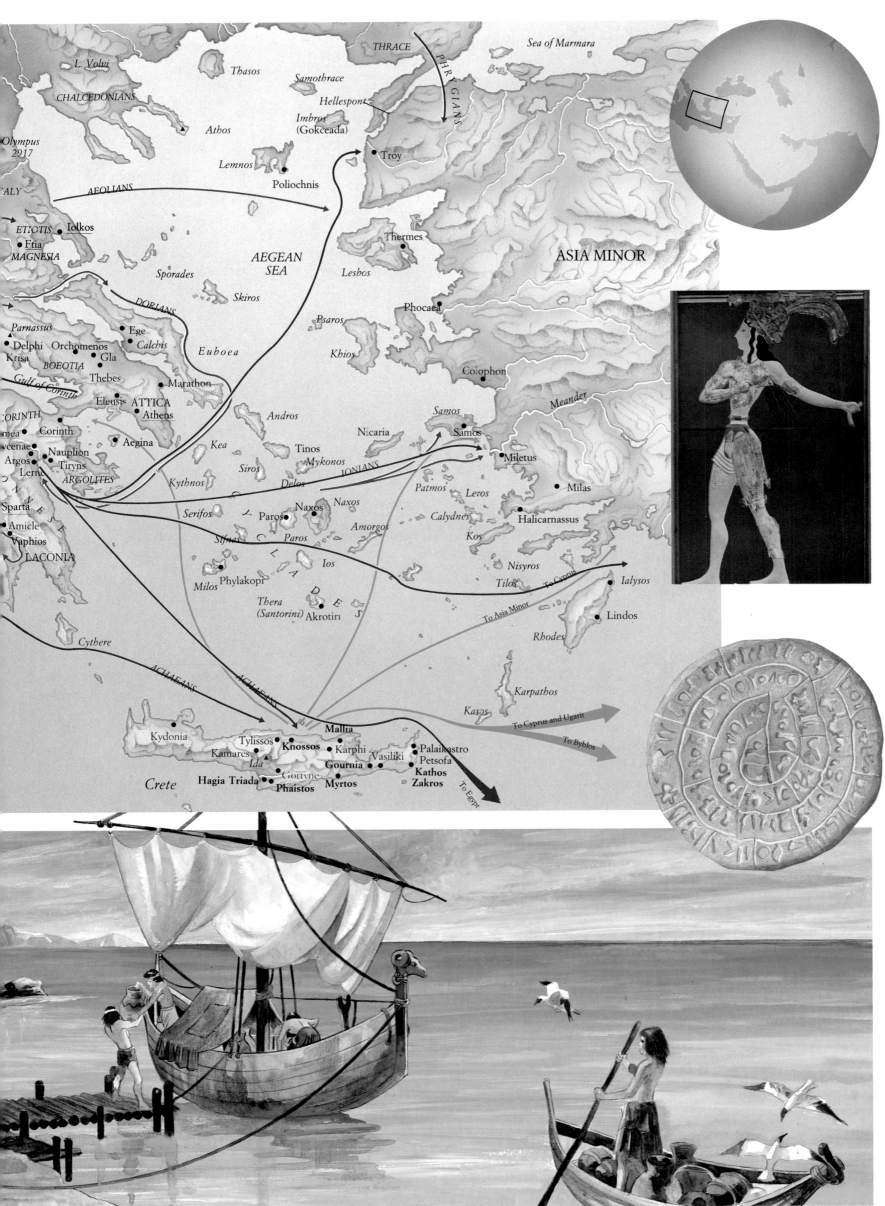

L. Volvi

CHALCEDONIANS

Thasos

Samothrace

THRACE

Sea of Marmara

PHRYGIANS

Hellespont

Imbros
(Gokceada)

Athos

Troy

Olympus
2917

Lemnos

Poliochnis

ITALY

AEOLIANS

ETIOTIS   Iolkos

Ftia

MAGNESIA

Sporades

Skiros

AEGEAN
SEA

Lesbos

Thermes

ASIA MINOR

Psaros

Khios

DORIANS

Parnassus

Ege   *Calchis*

Delphi   Orchomenos

Krisa   Gla

BOEOTIA   Thebes

Euboea

Phocaea

Colophon

Gulf of Corinth

Eleusis   Marathon

ATTICA

Meander

CORINTH   Athens

Andros

nea   Corinth

ycenae   Aegina

Argos   Nauplion

Lerna   Tiryns

ARGOLITES

Kea

Tinos

Mykonos

Siros

Kythnos

Delos

IONIANS

Samos

Samos

Miletus

Milas

Sparta

Nicaria

Serifos   Paros

Amicle

Vaphios

Sifnos

LACONIA

Paros

Naxos

Naxos

Amorgos

Patmos   Leros

Calydnes

Kos

Ios

Halicarnassus

Nisyros

Milos   Phylakopi

Thera
(Santorini)   Akrotiri

To Asia Minor

Tilos

To Cyprus

Ialysos

Lindos

Rhodes

Cythere

ACHAEANS

ACHAEANS

Karpathos

Kasos

To Cyprus and Ugarit

To Byblos

Kydonia

Mallia

Tylissos   Knossos

Kamares   Karphi

Ida   Vasiliki

Gournia

Hagia Triada   Gortyne

Phaistos   Myrtos

Palaikastro

Petsofa

Kathos

Zakros

To Egypt

Crete

29

7 THE AEGEAN CIVILIZATIONS

This marble statue of a harpist from about 2400 BC was found in a cemetery on a small island in the Cyclades.

The Bronze Age in the Aegean Sea region began about 3000 BC, and the culture that developed there had as its two main centres Knossos on the island of Crete and Mycenae. These two centres were at their peak for more than a thousand years, until between 1400 and 1000 BC.

Ancient origins

Before this period of advanced civilization, the peoples of Greece and the Aegean islands, including Crete, shared a common culture. The ancient Greeks called these early peoples 'Lelegi'. They were farmers, who benefited from fertile soil and a gentle climate.

About 2000 BC Indo-Europeans began to move into the Aegean; to the Greeks these were the Pelasgi. They had metal weapons and horses, and they overran the Aegean as easily as the Hittites had conquered Anatolia.

The importance of Crete

The Cyclades islands, which from Stone Age times had been a source of obsidian and an important trading centre for Mediterranean voyagers, were a meeting place for the interchange of cultures. During the Bronze Age, the centre of Aegean civilization shifted southwards to Crete. Crete already had links with Egypt, Asia Minor and the coastal towns of the eastern Mediterranean, such as Ugarit and Byblos.

Palaces and pigs

Between 2000 and 1650 BC the Cretans built splendid palaces, such as those at Knossos, Phaistos and Mallia. The palace was more than simply a grand home for a ruler; it was a centre of power and religious worship, a symbol of prestige and might. The Cretan palaces were not protected by stone walls, like the Hittite capital Hattusas. They had huge courtyards, with workshops, artists' studios, and storehouses for goods being shipped abroad, such as grain, oil, wine, timber and pottery, and for imported luxuries such as gold, ivory, precious stones and other fineries. Herds of cattle, sheep, goats, pigs and horses were reared in fields around the palaces.

Crete was a trading and cultural centre. Its rulers never sought to impose their will on others. They relied on the sea for defence, and as a means of contact with Greece and the other islands of the Aegean, as well as with Egypt, Cyprus and Mesopotamia.

Minoan Crete

In about 1700 BC, the palaces were destroyed by a natural disaster, probably an earthquake. But in a short time they were rebuilt, even more splendidly than before. Over the next two hundred years, the island was unified as one kingdom, with Knossos at its heart.

The scene below (pictured in colour on pages 28/29) shows Cretans going about their daily lives. For a thousand years these people enjoyed peace, with no need for walls around their cities. No enemy challenged their command of the sea, on which their wealth and security depended.

Here, men unload goods from a ship, and donkeys carry loads away inland. The Cretans were bold sailors, adventurers and merchants. They had skilled metalworkers and fine artists. From its position astride the sea routes of the eastern Mediterranean, Crete sent ships to fetch copper from Cyprus and tin from Spain, and with these two metals the island's smiths made bronze. The picture shows smiths at work around a smoking furnace melting tin and copper.

Most ordinary Cretans lived in villages dotted around the island, growing vines and olives on the fertile plains. The ruling families built their splendid palaces on the plains, too. Around them were workshops, and beyond them fields of crops.

This octopus floor decoration (left) comes from the palace of Nestor at Pilo, in the Peloponnese. The octopus was a popular subject in Minoan art.

The new Cretan culture was named after Minos, the legendary king of the island. It became known as 'Minoan'. From their palaces, the Minoans sent ships to trade across the Aegean Sea and with Egypt. Other peoples copied their art, especially their pottery. They also had a writing system, in which signs represented syllables. Minoan culture survived until the 1100s BC, but before then it had been taken over by another Aegean civilization, the Mycenaean.

Mycenae and Troy

Mycenae was a powerful city in mainland Greece. Its people developed a culture based on that of Crete. They copied Minoan palaces when building their own at Tiryns, Mycenae, Thebes and elsewhere. But, unlike the Cretans, they added immense stone walls for defence.

Another centre of Aegean culture was Troy. Here archaeologists have found the remains of nine cities, one of which (the seventh) was probably that described in the Greek stories about the Trojan War.

The Serpent Goddess (left) was a female idol. Throughout the Mediterranean, snakes were often associated with life-cycle beliefs. The goddess wears Cretan dress, with bare breasts and flounced skirt.

This vessel (below), held by a porcupine, is from the Cycladean island of Syros.

A Cretan statue (below) of a 'bird-god' riding a horse. It dates from between 1500 and 1000 BC.

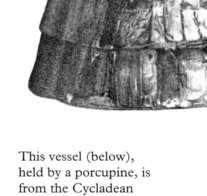

This clay model (left) of a covered wagon comes from northern Syria and dates from the second half of the third millennium BC. It is similar in design to the wagons used by the Scythians, who later invaded the Near East from the north.

This model of a war chariot (right) is also thought to have come from northern Syria. The horse-drawn chariot changed the way battles were fought.

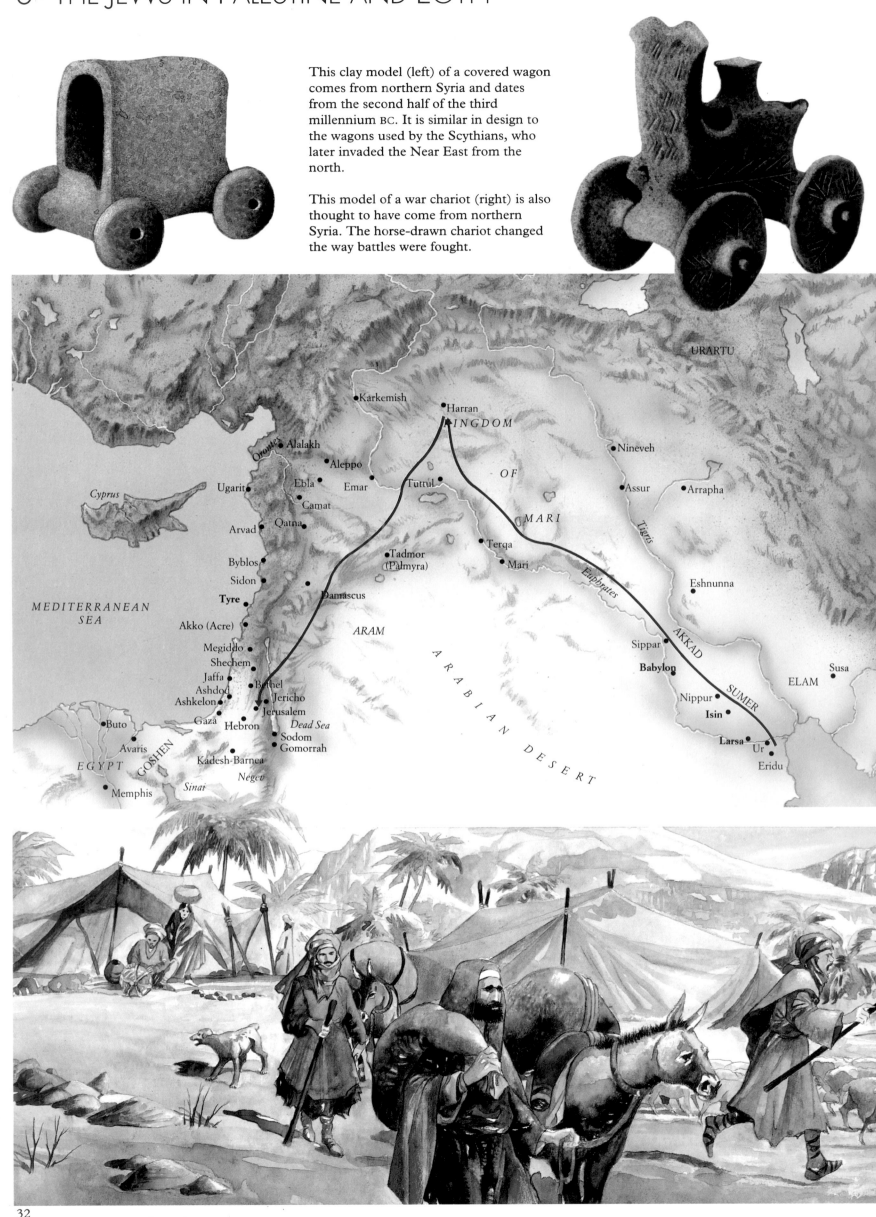

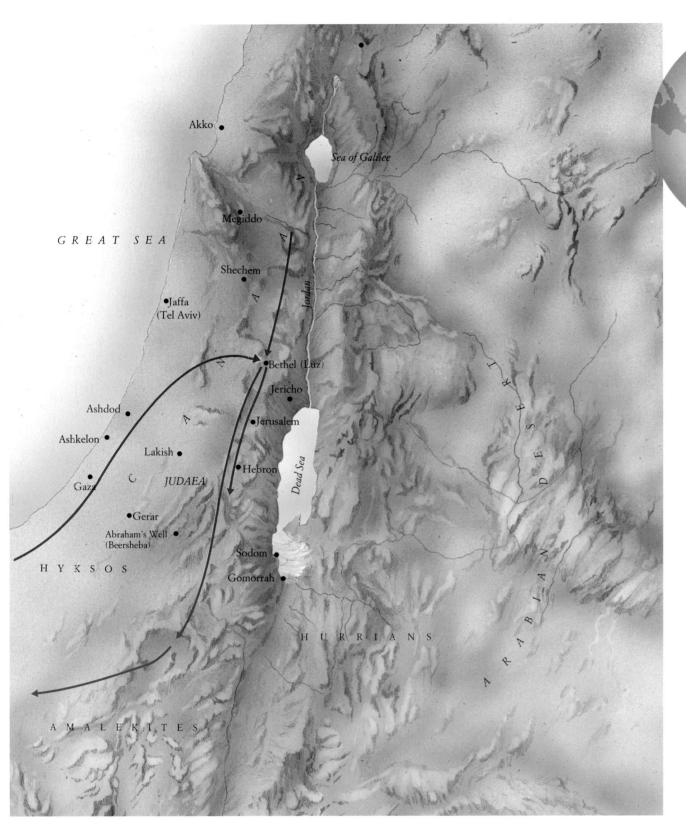

GREAT SEA

Akko

Sea of Galilee

Megiddo

Shechem

Jaffa
(Tel Aviv)

Bethel (Luz)

Jericho

Ashdod

Jerusalem

Ashkelon

Lakish

JUDAEA

Hebron

Dead Sea

Gaza

Gerar

Abraham's Well
(Beersheba)

Sodom

Gomorrah

HYKSOS

HURRIANS

ARABIAN DESERT

Jordan

AMALEKITES

The map on the opposite page shows the likely route taken by Terah (Abraham's father) from Ur to Harran, and Abraham's route on to the land of Canaan. The political upheaval after the collapse of the 3rd Dynasty of Ur (1955 BC) was probably the cause of these nomadic people leaving home, with their flocks, and following the Euphrates river north. They then turned south and east for Canaan. The map on this page shows Abraham's journey through Canaan (Palestine) into Egypt, and the return – which was forced on the nomads when drought dried up pastures in the Negev region.

8 The Jews in Palestine and Egypt

Mesopotamia came under Semitic influence before 2000 BC, when Sargon of Akkad reigned and extended his rule over much of Syria and Mesopotamia, uniting the various kingdoms around the Tigris and Euphrates rivers. The Akkadians were Semites, a group of peoples speaking related languages who could be found throughout the realm of King Sargon and on the outlying areas bordering the Fertile Crescent.

Wandering nomads

Many groups of nomads were on the move at this time, many of them entering Palestine and settling in Jordan and the Negev. Among these peoples were the Hebrews – the people from whom modern Jews are descended. The first information we have about them comes from the Books of Genesis and Numbers in the Bible, and from archaeological finds (such as the royal archives at Mari). These show that some time around 1800 BC a group of Hebrew nomads, led by Abraham, arrived in Canaan – later known as Palestine.

Abraham's journey

Abraham and his people set out from Ur in southern Mesopotamia. The first wave of emigration probably began as the Akkadians were moving in to the central and northern regions. Many groups set out, seeking new pasturelands. Abraham's father Terah was a leader. Among the travellers were his sons, including Abraham.

One group, or tribe, led by Abraham's brother Harran, settled in a land that was named Harran after him, and was perhaps near Mari.

Another group turned south and migrated to Canaan. With Abraham, leader of this group, was his nephew Lot. Lot is by tradition the founder of two peoples: the Moabites and the Ammonites, who settled east of Jordan

A stele from Ugarit (16th century BC), showing the god Baal brandishing a branch (to symbolize lightning). Baal was one of the gods the Hebrews encountered on their arrival in Palestine.

and south of the Dead Sea, founding the cities of Sodom and Gomorrah.

The Hebrews settled in the west of Palestine, but retained links with their old homeland in Mesopotamia. Some groups still lived as wandering nomads among the Judaean hills and the deserts of Sinai and the Negev. Others settled in villages.

The scene below (pictured in colour on pages 32/33) shows a caravan of Hebrew nomads travelling across Jordan on their way to Canaan.

The migrants took with them their sheep, donkeys and household goods. On the journey, they halted to graze their animals and grow crops. Often they paid taxes to the nearest town, trading with its inhabitants from their camp on the outskirts.

A town can be seen in the background. The travellers have made camp beside a waterhole, a precious green 'island' in the dusty, dry landscape. The picture shows the tents in which they lived, and which they took with them when they moved on, heading for the next watering place.

According to the Bible, Abraham was 75 when he left Harran and moved on towards Canaan – the Promised Land – to which he and his people believed their god would lead them.

These rock paintings (above) are from the central Negev. They show people dancing and playing musical instruments. The top picture shows two musicians with lyres (stringed instruments) and an animal. The bottom picture is of four dancers and a tambourine player. Such pictures, probably made by nomad shepherds in the 10th century BC, are found throughout the Sinai and Negev deserts.

The lineage of King David. Abraham, Isaac and Jacob are known in Hebrew literature as the Patriarchs. The sons of Jacob (who also adopted Joseph's sons Ephraim and Manasseh) gave their names to the Twelve Tribes of Israel.

The Hebrews in Egypt

The Hebrews settled in cities such as Jerusalem, Hebron, Beersheba and Gerar. They traded with the local inhabitants and moved about the countryside with their flocks, between wells and the rare rivers and streams. They made their living by selling wool and other produce of their sheep and goats, but also hunted and grew crops.

According to the Bible, the three central figures in this movement were Abraham, his son Isaac and his grandson Jacob. There were other leaders, too. The Hebrews brought with them their own god, but came to know the gods of Canaan – the chief of whom was known as El. The Hebrew religion was based on the worship of one god, a god of tribe, family and individual.

Jacob, Joseph and Moses

Jacob moved from Canaan to Egypt, probably during the reign of the Hyksos, when the city of Avaris in the Nile Delta became Egypt's capital. The Twelve Tribes of Israel (the Israelites) traced their descent from Jacob's 12 sons – one of whom, Joseph, had been sold into slavery in Egypt, but rose to be the Egyptian pharaoh's chief minister.

The Israelites remained in Egypt for over 400 years. With the removal of the Hyksos and the foundation of the New Kingdom (see pages 26/27), they were made slaves, but were eventually led out of Egypt by Moses (about 1200 BC), and returned to Canaan.

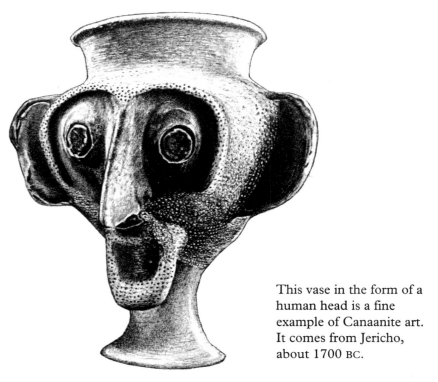

This vase in the form of a human head is a fine example of Canaanite art. It comes from Jericho, about 1700 BC.

9 EGYPT: MIDDLE AND NEW KINGDOMS

The map shows Egypt during the Middle and New Kingdoms, a period which began about 2040 BC. The arrows represent invasions by the Hyksos. The places in **bold** were capitals of Egypt during the dynasties listed below.

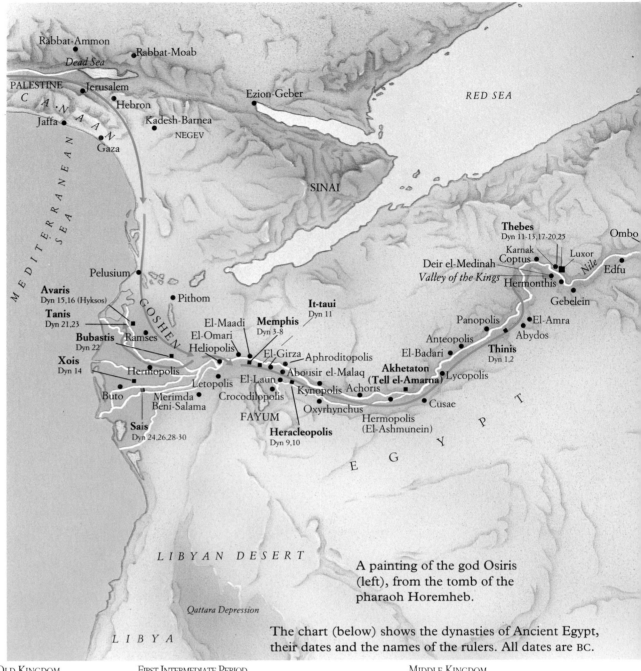

RED SEA

Rabbat-Ammon

Rabbat-Moab

Dead Sea

PALESTINE

Jerusalem

Hebron

Ezion-Geber

Jaffa

Kadesh-Barnea

Gaza

NEGEV

SINAI

MEDITERRANEAN SEA

Pelusium

Thebes
Dyn 11-13,17-20,25

Ombo

Karnak
Deir el-Medinah   Coptus   Luxor
Valley of the Kings

Nile   Edfu

Hermonthis

Avaris
Dyn 15,16 (Hyksos)

Pithom

Gebelein

Tanis
Dyn 21,23

GOSHEN

El-Maadi   **It-taui**
Dyn 11

Memphis
Dyn 3-8

Panopolis   El-Amra

Bubastis
Dyn 22

Ramses

El-Omari
Heliopolis

El-Girza

Anteopolis   Abydos

El-Badari   **Thinis**
Dyn 1,2

Xois
Dyn 14

Hermopolis

Letopolis

El-Laun

Aphroditopolis

Abousir el-Malaq   **Akhetaton**
(**Tell el-Amarna**)

Lycopolis

Buto

Merimda
Beni-Salama

Crocodilopolis

Kynopolis   Achoris

Cusae

Sais
Dyn 24,26,28-30

FAYUM   **Heracleopolis**
Dyn 9,10

Oxyrhynchus

Hermopolis
(El-Ashmunein)

E G Y P T

LIBYAN DESERT

A painting of the god Osiris (left), from the tomb of the pharaoh Horemheb.

Qattara Depression

L I B Y A

The chart (below) shows the dynasties of Ancient Egypt, their dates and the names of the rulers. All dates are BC.

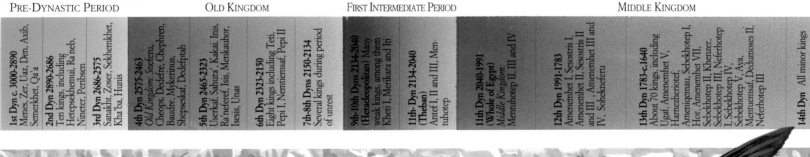

PRE-DYNASTIC PERIOD		OLD KINGDOM		FIRST INTERMEDIATE PERIOD		MIDDLE KINGDOM		

1st Dyn c. 3000-2890 Menes, Zer, Uaz, Den, Axib, Semerkhet, Qa'a

2nd Dyn 2890-2686 Ten kings, including Hetepsekhemui, Ra neb, Nineter, Peribsen

3rd Dyn 2686-2575 Sanakht, Zoser, Sekhemkhet, Kha'ba, Hunis

4th Dyn 2575-2465 *Old Kingdom:* Snefery, Cheops, Dedefre, Chephren, Baudre, Mykerinus, Shepseskaf, Dedefptah

5th Dyn 2465-2323 Userkaf, Sahura', Kakai, Inis, Ra neferef, Isis, Menkauhor, Isesis, Unas

6th Dyn 2323-2150 Teti, Pepi I, Nemtiemsaf, Pepi II

7th-8th Dyns 2150-2134 Several kings during period of unrest

9th-10th Dyns 2134-2040 (Heracleopolitan) Many weak kings, among them Kheti I, Merikara and Iti

11th Dyn 2134-2040 (Theban) Antef I, II and III, Men-tuhotep

11th Dyn 2040-1991 (Whole of Egypt) *Middle Kingdom:* Mentuhotep II, III and IV

12th Dyn 1991-1783 Amenemhet I, Sesostris I, Amenemhet II, Sesostris II and III , Amenemhet III and IV, Sobekneferu

13th Dyn 1783-c.1640 About 70 kings, including Ugaf, Amenemhet V, Harnezheriotef, Amenigemau, Sebekhotep I, Hor, Amenemhet VII, Sebekhotep II, Khenzer, Sebekhotep III, Neferhotep I, Sebekhotep IV, Sebekhotep V, Aya, Mentuemsaf, Dedumoses II, Neferhotep III

14th Dyn All minor kings

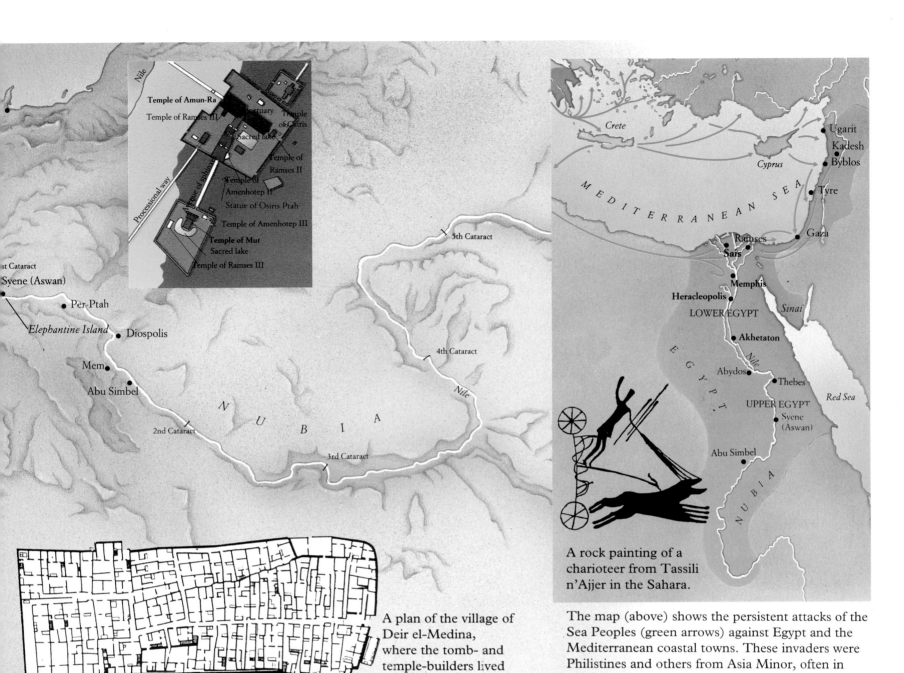

Temple of Amun-Ra
Temple of Ramses III
Sanctuary
Temple of Osiris
Sacred lake
Processional way
Avenue of sphinxes
Temple of Ramses II
Temple of Amenhotep II
Statue of Osiris Ptah
Temple of Amenhotep III
Temple of Mut
Sacred lake
Temple of Ramses III

Nile

5th Cataract
4th Cataract
3rd Cataract
2nd Cataract
1st Cataract
Syene (Aswan)
Per-Ptah
Elephantine Island
Diospolis
Mem
Abu Simbel
N U B I A
Nile

Crete
M E D I T E R R A N E A N   S E A
Cyprus
Ugarit
Kadesh
Byblos
Tyre
Gaza
Ramses
Sais
Memphis
Heracleopolis
LOWER EGYPT
Sinai
Akhetaton
Abydos
Thebes
E G Y P T
UPPER EGYPT
Syene (Aswan)
Red Sea
Abu Simbel
N U B I A

A rock painting of a charioteer from Tassili n'Ajjer in the Sahara.

A plan of the village of Deir el-Medina, where the tomb- and temple-builders lived crowded together.

The map (above) shows the persistent attacks of the Sea Peoples (green arrows) against Egypt and the Mediterranean coastal towns. These invaders were Philistines and others from Asia Minor, often in alliance with Libyans.

SECOND INTERMEDIATE PERIOD			NEW KINGDOM			THIRD INTERMEDIATE PERIOD					LATE PERIOD		
15th Dyn 1640-1532 Hyksos kings	**16th Dyn** Minor Hyksos kings	**17th Dyn 1645-1567** Many Theban kings: Antef V, Sebekemsaf I, Nebirierau, Sebekemsaf II, Ta o I and II, Kamose	**18th Dyn 1567-1307** *New Kingdom:* Ahmose, Amenhotep I, Thutmose I, II and III, Hatshepsut, Amenhotep II, Thutmose IV, Amenhotep III and IV (Akhenaten), Smenkhkar (Nefertiti?) Tutankhamun, Ay, Horemheb	**19th Dyn 1307-1196** Ramses I, Seti I, Ramses II, Merneptah, Seti II, Amenmeses (usurper), Siptah, Tuosre	**20th Dyn 1196-1070** Setnakht, Ramses III, IV, V, VI, VII, VIII, IX, X and XI	**21st Dyn 1070-945** Smendes, Amenemnisu, Psusenna I, Amenemope, Osorkon I, Siamon, PsusennaII	**22nd Dyn 945-712** Sheshonq I, Osorkon II, Takelot I, Sheshonq II, Osorkon III, Takelot II, Sheshonq III, Pami, Sheshonq V, Osorkon V	**23rd Dyn c.828-712** Succession of kings crowned at Thebes, Hermopolis, Heracleopolis, Leontopolis and Tanis	**24th Dyn 724-712 (Bochoris Sais)** Tefnakhe,	**25th Dyn 770-712 (Nubia and Thebes)** Kashta, Piankhi	**25th Dyn 712-657 (Nubia and the whole of Egypt)** Shabaka, Shebitku, Taharqa, Tantamani	**26th Dyn 664-525** Necho I, Psamtik I, Necho II, Psamtik II, Apries, Amasis, Psamtik III	**27th Dyn 525-404** Persian kings through conquest

28th- 30th Dyn 404-343 Last independent dynasties before Persian and Greek rulers

9 EGYPT: MIDDLE AND NEW KINGDOMS

The kings of the 11th Dynasty (2040-1991 BC) re-established their control over all of Egypt. This victory marks the beginning of what historians call the Middle Kingdom. Their success was built on by the 12th-Dynasty rulers Amenemhet I and Sesóstris III, who occupied Nubia, Palestine and Phoenicia (Lebanon), and encouraged contacts with Crete, where Minoan civilization was in full bloom.

Too many rulers, and another enemy
But with seventy or so rulers in 150 years, Egypt's power over its empire again weakened and Asian peoples settled in the eastern Nile Delta. To make things worse, in about 1640 BC the Hyksos moved into Lower Egypt.

The invaders had horses and war chariots, and were strong enough to found their own dynasties in Egypt, ruling as pharaohs. They ruled from Avaris (later Tanis) in the Nile Delta.

The New Kingdom
During the 1500s BC the Egyptians regained the upper hand, under the pharaohs Kamose and Ahmose (who were brothers). They drove the Hyksos out, and the new Egypt became very much a military state.

It was an empire now, not a kingdom, for its rulers controlled Kush, Nubia and Syria. Thutmose I fought as far east as the Euphrates. He was the first pharaoh to be buried in the Valley of the Kings, the great burial place on the west bank of the Nile opposite Thebes. Some historians think he was the greatest of all Egyptian pharaohs.

Akhenaten's reign and religious battles
In this new Egypt, the high priests of Egypt's religion held great power. They ordered the building of massive temples and conducted awe-inspiring rituals. Huge statues like the Colossi of Memnon (raised in Amenhotep III's honour) were erected.

Amenhotep's son, Amenhotep IV, challenged priestly power. He renamed himself Akhenaten, meaning 'he who brought favour to the sun' and tried to set up a new religion. He built a new capital at Tell el-Amarna (Akhetaton) and tried to end the old worship of the god Amun. When he died, his reforms were overthrown and his new capital demolished. His son-in-law was the short-reigned pharaoh Tutankhamun, whose tomb and burial treasures were found by archaeologists in 1922, perfectly preserved in the Valley of the Kings.

The village scene (pictured in colour on pages 36/37) shows a labourers' village called Deir el-Medina. It was near the Valleys of the Kings and Queens, where many of the kings and queens of Egypt were entombed, near Thebes.

These workers dug and decorated the tombs of the kings.

Their village was abandoned in the 11th century BC and covered by sand.

The tomb-builders lived in villages beside the Nile, enclosed by walls of mud and brick, which protected the warehouses crammed with valuable building materials and stores. Tomb-building was a mystery, to be

hidden from prying eyes, and security was probably tight.

The women did the farming, while the men worked as labourers, stone-carvers, painters or scribes. The women grew wheat to make bread, and barley for beer.

The village was made up of rows of small, narrow houses,

with four rooms for one family. The flat roofs were used as work-spaces – people could chat across the street as they worked. Through the dusty streets, donkeys carried water from the Nile and produce from the irrigated fields.

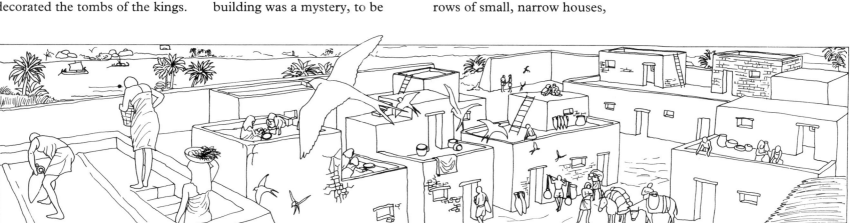

The sun disc of Aton (opposite page) radiates divine protection over Akhenaten and his family. This limestone stele is from a household altar at El-Amarna.

A black basalt head of Pharaoh Ramses II, wearing the crown of Upper Egypt.

The Egyptians used light war chariots (below) with four-spoked wheels, pulled by two horses. These chariots were fast when skilfully handled.

This enamelled ankh, or T-shaped cross (left), bears the symbol of the god Osiris, and a dog-headed sceptre. Only kings, queens and gods were allowed to wear the ankh, the symbol of life.

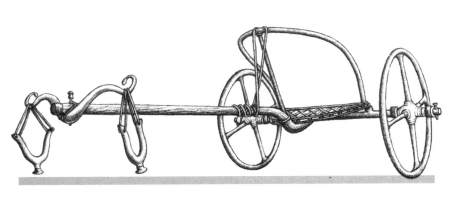

Wars, invasions and foreign rule

Seti II (1307-1290 BC) and Ramses II (1290-1224 BC) led the Egyptians in wars against the Hittites. Ramses II's heir was Merneptah, who built a new capital in the Delta (possibly at modern Qantir). He fought against invading Libyans and the Sea Peoples – a confederation of invaders from the Mediterranean including peoples from Italy, the Aegean and Greece.

The Sea Peoples were looking for land. They marched ashore with their families and goods following in wagons, while their ships advanced along the coast. Ramses III (1194-1163 BC) drove back their forces, although many of the invaders settled outside Egypt's borders. After Ramses III, a succession of weak kings allowed the Libyans to advance once more and they set up their own dynasty, the 22nd in the long line of Egypt's ruling houses.

Egypt's great days were coming to an end. But the empire was still a glorious prize for conquest. In the last 700 years BC, Egypt was successively occupied by Assyrians, Persians, Greeks (Alexander the Great's Macedonians) and finally the Romans.

The god Bes (below), grotesque protector of the family, pokes out his tongue while dancing on a lotus flower and beating a tambourine.

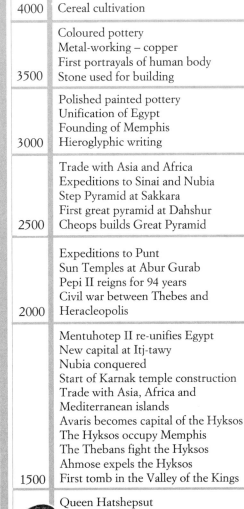

TIME CHART OF ANCIENT EGYPT

4000	Cereal cultivation
3500	Coloured pottery Metal-working – copper First portrayals of human body Stone used for building
3000	Polished painted pottery Unification of Egypt Founding of Memphis Hieroglyphic writing
2500	Trade with Asia and Africa Expeditions to Sinai and Nubia Step Pyramid at Sakkara First great pyramid at Dahshur Cheops builds Great Pyramid
2000	Expeditions to Punt Sun Temples at Abur Gurab Pepi II reigns for 94 years Civil war between Thebes and Heracleopolis
1500	Mentuhotep II re-unifies Egypt New capital at Itj-tawy Nubia conquered Start of Karnak temple construction Trade with Asia, Africa and Mediterranean islands Avaris becomes capital of the Hyksos The Hyksos occupy Memphis The Thebans fight the Hyksos Ahmose expels the Hyksos First tomb in the Valley of the Kings
1000	Queen Hatshepsut Thutmose III conquers Syria Start of Luxor temples' construction Akhenaten founds the city of Akhetaton Tutankhamun returns to Thebes Conflict with the Hittites in Syria Merneptah repels Libyan assaults Ramses III pushes back Sea Peoples Building of royal tombs at Thebes
500	Theban priests enjoy greatest power Sheshonq I sacks Jerusalem Kushite king governs Egypt Assyrian invasions Founding of Greek colonies in Egypt The Persians annex Egypt

10 THE PHOENICIANS AND MEDITERRANEAN NAVIGATION

During the reign of the Egyptian pharaoh Necho (609-593 BC), Phoenician ships explored the coasts of Africa (below). Their voyages took them as far south as Punt (Ethiopia/Somalia) and Ophir (Zimbabwe/Mozambique) with whom Egypt traded.

The main map shows the commercial and colonizing activities of the Phoenicians during the 1st millennium BC. They were to be found across the Mediterranean, from east to west.

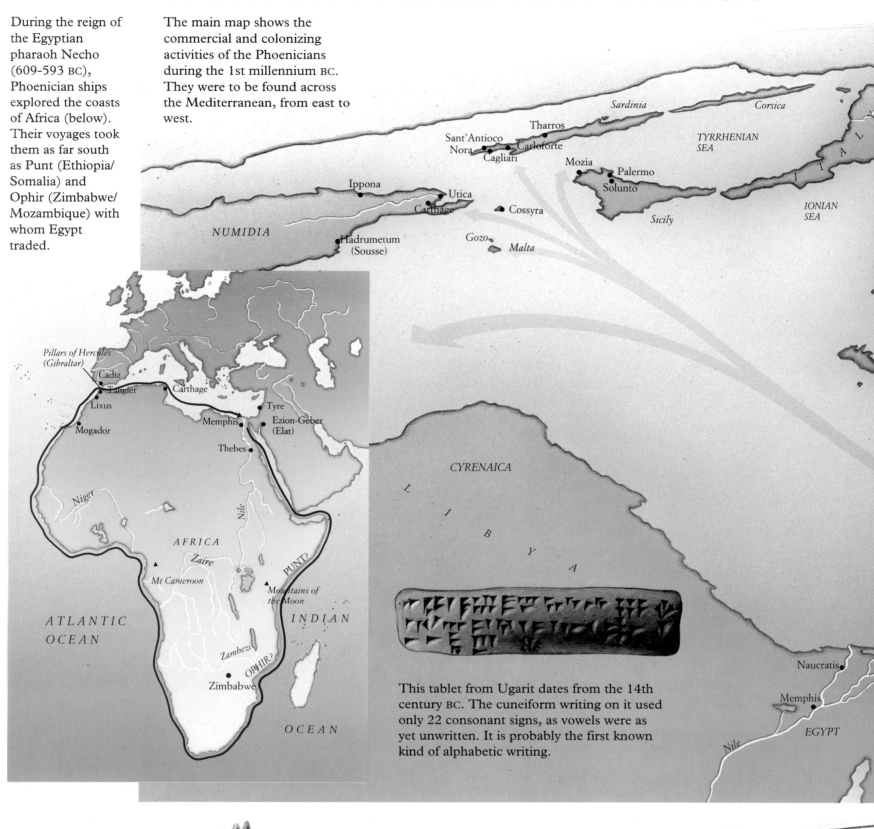

This tablet from Ugarit dates from the 14th century BC. The cuneiform writing on it used only 22 consonant signs, as vowels were as yet unwritten. It is probably the first known kind of alphabetic writing.

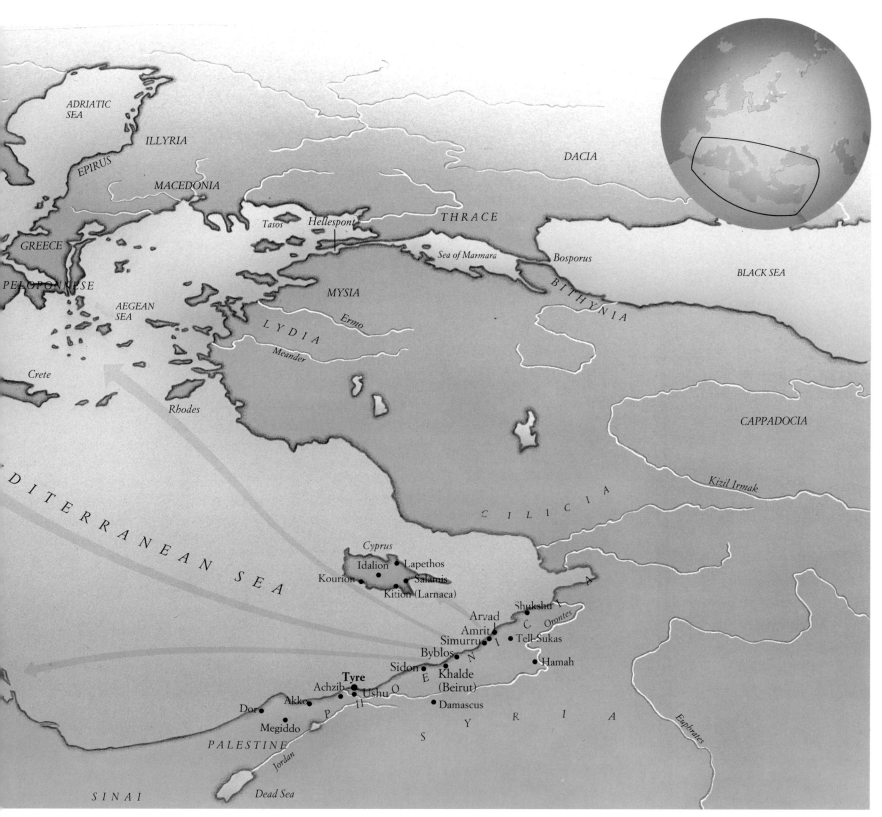

ADRIATIC SEA

ILLYRIA

EPIRUS

MACEDONIA

DACIA

GREECE

PELOPONNESE

AEGEAN SEA

Crete

Rhodes

Tasos

Hellespont

THRACE

Sea of Marmara

Bosporus

BLACK SEA

MYSIA

Ermo

LYDIA

Meander

BITHYNIA

CAPPADOCIA

Kizil Irmak

C I L I C I A

MEDITERRANEAN SEA

Cyprus

Idalion   Lapethos

Kourion   Salamis

Kition (Larnaca)

Shukshu

Arvad

Amrit   Orontes

Simurru   Tell-Sukas

Byblos

Sidon   Hamah

Khalde
(Beirut)

Tyre

Achzib   Ushu

Akko   Damascus

Dor

Megiddo

PALESTINE

Jordan

SINAI   Dead Sea

S Y R I A

Euphrates

10 THE PHOENICIANS AND MEDITERRANEAN NAVIGATION

An enigmatic smile: this woman's face was carved on a piece of wooden furniture. The Phoenicians loved decoration, even on everyday objects.

Around 1200 BC, as the Bronze Age gave way to the Iron Age around the shores of the Mediterranean, the Sea Peoples invaded Canaan (Syria and Palestine), and drove out the great Egyptian and Mesopotamian powers. They overcame the Israelites, the Aramaeans, and other weaker states in the area. The coastal Canaan cities were now free to govern themselves. This was not something new. The city of Byblos had flourished during the 3rd and 2nd millennia BC. Though tied to Egypt, it had independent links with Ebla and Mari. At the beginning of the 11th century BC, Byblos became the first coastal city to re-establish its importance after the disruption caused by the Sea Peoples.

The Phoenicians

The Canaanites, as they are called in the Old Testament of the Bible, lived on the coastal strip of what are now Syria, Lebanon and Israel, roughly from Shukshu in the north to Akko in the south. They were named *Phoenikes* by the Greeks, from the Greek word *phoinix* (meaning purple-red). This was the colour of the dye they used to transform the natural shades of the cloth they made. We now call this colour Tyrian purple.

Sidon and Tyre

In the first period of Phoenician civilization (1200-1000 BC), biblical sources indicate that Sidon held some sway over the other coastal cities. Indeed the Phoenicians were often called Sidonians. But after 1000 BC, the same sources (the Old Testament books of Kings and Ezekial) give prominence to Tyre, the Phoenician port that had close trade links with the kingdom of Israel. In exchange for corn, oil, wine and other farm produce essential to the maritime city's survival, Hiram, king of Tyre (c.969-936 BC), sent gold and silver, cedar wood and pine, builders and labourers to help King Solomon in the construction of the Temple in Jerusalem. Together the two rulers built up a fleet that sailed from Eilat on the Red Sea coast as far as Ophir, carrying gold, perfumes and precious woods. At the same time, Hiram quelled a rebellion at Kition, showing that Tyre also had a footing on the island of Cyprus.

Merchant voyagers

From the 9th century BC onwards, the Phoenicians dominated trade in the Aegean. Their ships sailed to Rhodes, Crete and the Dodecanese and even as far as Cilicia and Anatolia, where they acquired silver, iron and tin. Then, between the end of the 9th century BC and the beginning of the 8th, the formation of a strong Aramaic state in Damascus and the foundation of Greek colonies in Cilicia closed this northern trade area to Phoenician merchants. Tyre turned to the west, especially Iberia (Spain), where it could obtain good supplies of gold, silver and tin. To voyage across the Mediterranean was such a large undertaking that

The port of Tyre (pictured in colour on pages 40/41) is, as always, busy and prosperous. On the quayside, people wait to celebrate the return from the high seas of a convoy of ships. Phoenicia's ships bring metals and cereals from distant Iberia (Spain), or from the many trading bases in the central and eastern Mediterranean. For a maritime city such as Tyre, with no agricultural land, trade is essential, especially the more lucrative long-distance trade.

On the left, a ship has been beached for repairs. Ships arrive regularly to be overhauled, caulked, remasted and rigged. No sailor wants to risk losing a single load of wine, oil, pottery or Tyrian purple cloth, the goods seen being checked on the right. These shrewd and far-sighted merchants guard their reputations as seafarers and their profits as traders.

A *Murex* shell. This mollusc was the source of the Tyrian purple dye.

A Phoenician war galley, used for defending the trade routes between the colonies and trading posts.

it was not feasible without the backing of a great power like Assyria. The Assyrians guaranteed the sale of all the goods they bought. Tyre in fact acted as agent for all Assyrian long-distance trade. This period can be described as 'pre-colonization'. Although ancient histories tell of Phoenician colonies (Lixus, Utica and Cadiz) in the 12th century BC, the only archaeological evidence of colonies comes from the 7th century BC.

Navigation

It is not thought that in the last few thousand years Mediterranean currents have suddenly changed course, nor the winds their direction. Depending on the time of the year, Phoenician sailors travelling between Tyre and Cadiz in Spain would have had a choice of two routes. The simplest was the southern route: Egypt-Libya-North East Africa. Coastal navigation was always possible by day on this route. The ships could cover about 40 kilometres (25 miles) and then stop for the night. On the longer northern route: Cyprus-Anatolia-Aegean-Malta-Sicily-Sardinia-Balearic Islands, the ships sailed at night, using the stars to find their way. Their crews orientated themselves by observing the position of the Little Bear constellation, whose brightest star, the Pole Star, was known in ancient times as the Phoenician Star. Often ships were blown off course as they approached Sicily, Sardinia and the Balearic Islands, but Motya, Tharros and Ibiza were compulsory ports of call. The passage through the Straits of Gibraltar was tricky and dangerous. Often it was preferable to transport goods overland along the road from Cadiz to Malaga.

Carthage

Carthage, one of the first Phoenician colonies (traditionally founded in 813-814 BC), was not just a stopping-off place. Its name means 'new city'. (Utica, which dates from 1101 BC, means 'old city'.) Carthage together with other nearby colonies in the eastern Mediterranean made up an area called the 'Phoenician triangle'. They kept out the Etruscans and fought the Greeks for control of the sea, making the triangle virtually impregnable.

Meaning	Sound	Canaanite of Sinai c. 1500 BC	Phoenician c. 1000 BC	Old Hebrew c. 700 BC	Aramaic c. 500 BC	Hebrew 1st century AD	Ancient Greek c. 600 BC	Classical Greek 5th century AD
cattle	A							A
house	B							B
palm of hand	K							K
group	L							Γ
water	M							M
eye	O							O
head	R							R

At the end of the 10th century BC, Assyria started to expand again, after the Aramaic raids which had greatly reduced its activities. Under the rule of Shalmaneser III, the Assyrians reached the Euphrates. The map shows Assyrian territory under Assur-dan II (934–912 BC) and its further expansion under Shalmaneser III, who undertook a wider range of conquests. The Assyrian rulers were keen to record their military campaigns in annals and on monuments. They were great believers in propaganda to enhance their fearsome reputations.

PLAN OF ASSUR

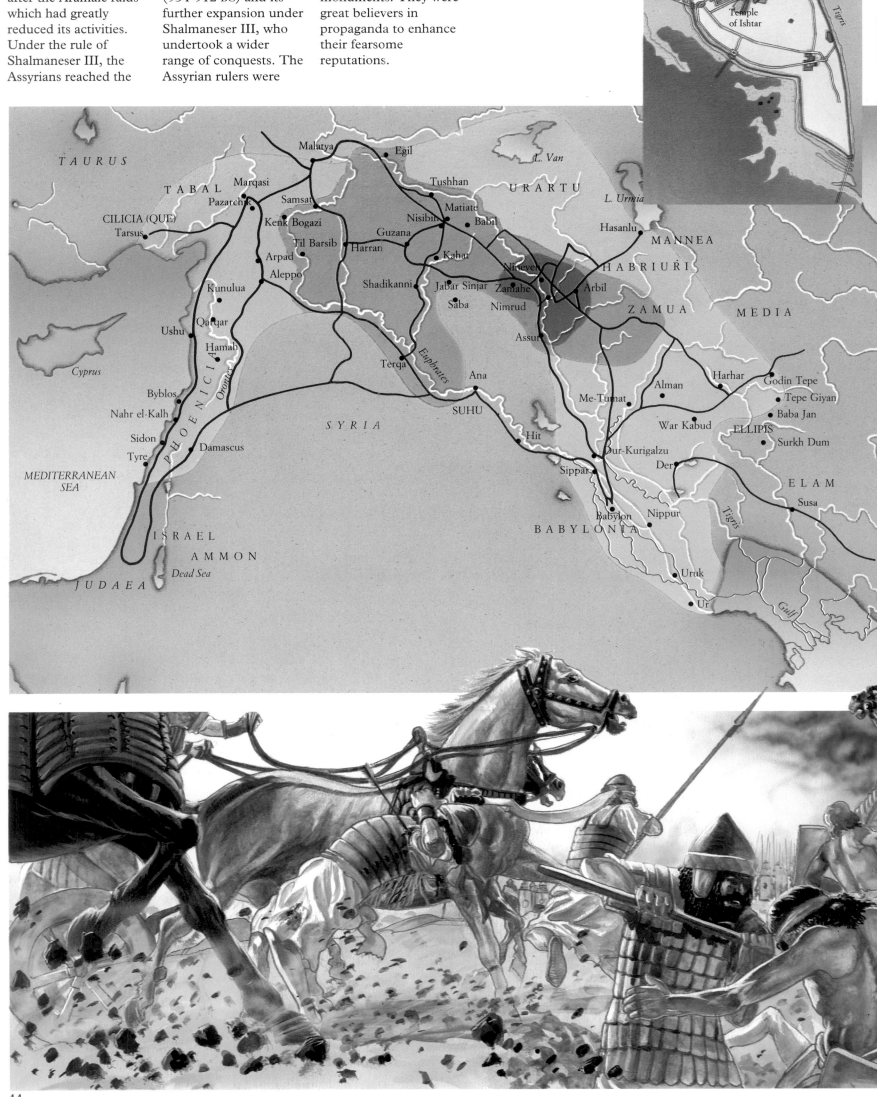

TAURUS

TABAL

CILICIA (QUE)

Tarsus

Marqasi

Pazarchik

Samsat

Kenk Bogazi

Til Barsib

Arpad

Aleppo

Kunulua

Qarqar

Ushu

Hamah

Byblos

Nahr el-Kalb

Sidon

Tyre

MEDITERRANEAN SEA

Cyprus

Orontes

PHOENICIA

Damascus

ISRAEL

AMMON

Dead Sea

JUDAEA

Malatya

Egil

Tushhan

Matiate

Nisibin

Babil

Guzana

Harran

Kahat

Shadikanni

Jabar Sinjar

Saba

Terqa

Euphrates

Ana

SUHU

SYRIA

Hit

L. Van

URARTU

L. Urmia

Hasanlu

Nineveh

Zamahe

Arbil

Nimrud

Assur

MANNEA

HABRIURI

ZAMUA

MEDIA

Me-Turnat

Alman

War Kabud

Dur-Kurigalzu

Sippar

Babylon

Nippur

BABYLONIA

Harhar

Godin Tepe

Tepe Giyan

Baba Jan

ELLIPIS

Surkh Dum

Der

Tigris

ELAM

Susa

Uruk

Ur

Gulf

A detail from a 7th-century BC bas-relief from Nineveh, showing a mounted warrior apparently making a proclamation.

Gilgamesh was a legendary Sumerian hero, the subject of the first long epic poem known to history. This 8th-century BC relief (right) comes from Khorsabad, the Assyrian capital founded by Sargon II. It shows Gilgamesh with a captured lion.

The kingdom of Urartu (below). The Urartians, who came from the harsh Armenian mountains, were Assyria's chief rivals. In the 8th century BC, the domain of Urartu, with its capital at Tushpa, stretched from Lake Van, its original stronghold, to lakes Urmia and Sevan.

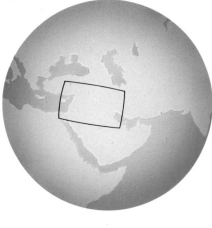

The Assyrian empire at its greatest extent, which came under the rule of Asarhaddon and Assurbanipal, who around the middle of the 7th century BC conquered Egypt and Elam for a short time. In 612 BC, the Assyrians ceded power to the rebuilt kingdom of Babylon and the Medes, or Medians.

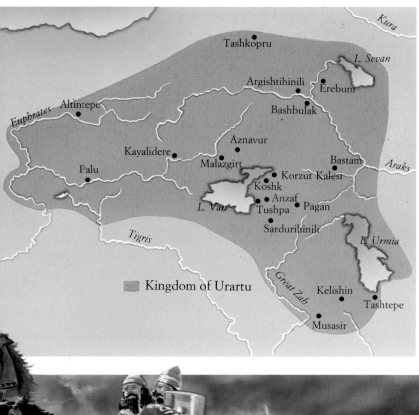

Kingdom of Urartu

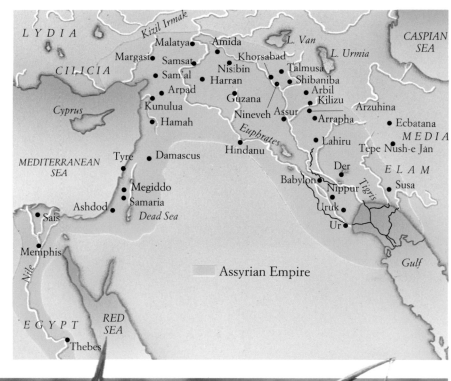

Assyrian Empire

11 THE ASSYRIAN EMPIRE

The Assyrians were the direct heirs of the Sumerian-Babylonian civilization, which they absorbed and copied. They distinguished themselves mainly by their prowess in war, and the violent devastation of their enemies.

The wars of Tiglathpileser I

Tiglathpileser I (1114-1076 BC), was the first Assyrian king to extend the empire. He waged a violent war against the Babylonians to the south, and in the upper valley of the Tigris, defeated a strong Phrygian force. By invading and occupying the Anatolian plains, he probably brought about the end of the Hittite kingdom.

To the west, he fought against the Aramaeans, pushing beyond the Euphrates as far as the Mediterranean. His conquests disintegrated on his death, and in the following centuries, Assyria returned to its old 8th-century borders – the territory made up of Assur, Nineveh and Arbil, newly divided into small city-states.

In the following three centuries, although there is evidence of Assyrian involvement with the west, Tiglathpileser's successors kept largely to themselves. Although weakened, Assyria was left unharmed by the turbulent years of decline at the end of the 2nd millennium BC, which had affected even Egypt and Greece. From the end of the 10th century BC, under Adad-nirari II (911-891 BC) and his heirs, Assyria began to expand again, mainly in the west, and once more reached the Euphrates.

Assurnasirpal's expansion

Assurnasirpal II (883-859 BC) turned his attention to the north, east and south. The most successful outcome of his military campaigns was against the weak city-states of Syria

A fragment from an ivory slab shows a warrior struggling with a lion. He fends off the beast's jaws with his shield and stabs it with his spear.

and Palestine, governed by local rulers. In 877 BC, he reached the shores of the 'Great Sea of the Land of the Ammurians' – the Mediterranean. More than just military conquests, these victories served to widen Assyria's influence and place many formerly independent rulers under its protection and control.

Assurnasirpal's son, Shalmaneser III (858-254 BC) pushed Assyria's boundaries to the east bank of the Euphrates, and fought against a coalition of weaker states (including Damascus, Israel and Egypt) to force them to pay tribute. Thirty years of war gave him control of Que (Cilicia) and the northern states of the Taurus (Turkey), with the trade routes for silver and marble.

On his death, there was a power struggle between his sons, and as a result Assyria became weaker. Tiglathpileser III (744-727 BC) restored the old supremacy, and by the

The Assyrians at war (pictured in colour on pages 44/45). By the time the Assyrians turned to the conquest of Asia Minor and Mesopotamia, they had perfected the art of warfare and systematic extermination. Ferocious and merciless, they crushed subject peoples who tried to rebel. They burnt and sacked cities, devastated the countryside, tortured prisoners or carried them off to slavery in their thousands.

An Assyrian king wrote in his *Annals* : 'I have smashed the enemy land like a pot and I have reduced its capital like a flood. I have impaled the king on the city gate and I have deported his people, his wife and children, and taken his worldly goods'.

The Assyrian armies were the best organized of their day. The officers came from an aristocracy deeply loyal to the sovereign. The infantry was made up of archers and spearmen who defended themselves with large shields, armour and helmets. The cavalry charged into battle in armoured war chariots, driven by a charioteer and carrying a heavily armed warrior. For attacking towns, the Assyrians developed ingenious siege machinery.

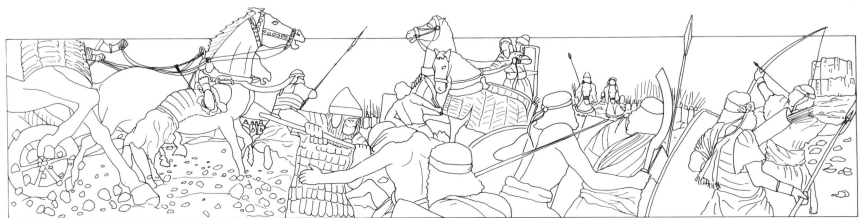

Lion-hunting was a popular recreation for the king. This bas-relief shows a hunt at the palace of Assurnasirpal II at Nimrud (ancient Kalkhu), the city he chose as capital. The king points his bow towards the lion, which is being driven up to him by beaters.

THE KINGDOM OF URARTU Northwards, Assyrian expansion was always blocked by Urartu. This kingdom stretched around Lake Van, in the rugged mountains where Turkey, Iraq, Iran, Armenia and Georgia have their borders today. Its culture had many Assyrian characteristics but it remained independent. It had a mainly agricultural economy, but also specialized in bronze and iron working. In the 9th century BC, the Urartians, sheltered by the almost insurmountable southerly mountains, expanded north to Lake Sevan, east to Lake Urmia and west to the Euphrates. Only in 716 BC did a conflict between the king of Urartu and the state of Mannea (in western Iran), a vassal of the Assyrians, give Sargon II the opportunity to conduct a victorious, if indecisive, campaign against the mountain people. The threat of the Cimmerians advancing from southern Russia, however, led the two warring states to adopt peaceful relations, which were maintained for a hundred years.

end of his reign the list of tax-paying regions included Syria, Phoenicia, Israel, Judah and Ammon. His son Shalmaneser V became ruler of Babylon, conquered Samaria and deported the Israelites.

In 722 BC, in obscure circumstances, Sargon II became ruler of Assyria. Revolts in Damascus, Samaria and Gaza gave him the opportunity to expand his rule to the Egyptian border. He went on to annex Babylon in 709 BC. Sargon was killed in battle in the Taurus Mountains in 705 BC, and succeeded by his son Sennacherib.

Sennacherib and later rulers

During his 24-year rule, Sennacherib (704-680 BC), did not extend Assyria's empire. Instead he had to fight to suppress rebellions. In 701 BC he marched against Syria and Palestine. On the Philistine plains, he fought the Egyptians who were aiding the rebels. In 703 BC Babylon rebelled, was besieged and eventually destroyed in 689 BC. Sennacherib rebuilt Nineveh before being killed there by one of his sons.

The next ruler of Assyria was Esarhaddon (680–688 BC), who conquered Memphis in Egypt, and with booty carried back, rebuilt Babylon.

Esarhaddon was followed by Assurbanipal, who reconquered Egypt after two campaigns (667 and 664 BC). He then fought his brother, who ruled Babylon. When he died, with Babylon again quelled, the turbulent city again rose in revolt. This uprising provoked the collapse of Assyria. The second Babylonian empire had begun.

A bas-relief of Sargon II (above). Pictures of Assyrian kings all look so like each other that they are difficult to identify if there are no inscriptions.

A tripod and cauldron from Urartu, made of bronze and decorated with bulls' heads. Urartian artisans were masters of metalwork.

The Assyrian army was made up of conscripts forcibly enlisted from the ever-increasing ranks of defeated soldiers and prisoners. A special corps was made up of slingers (stone-throwers) who covered the advance of the spearmen.

12 THE BIRTH OF ISRAEL

The Hebrew kingdom formed by King David received tribute from neighbouring vassal states that had been conquered. Under King Solomon, the Hebrew state enjoyed a period of great splendour.

The main map shows the Bible lands. The red line shows one of the possible routes of the Jewish exodus from Egypt. Biblical, historical and archaeological studies have all tried to find the true facts about the story of the 'chosen people' who left Egypt in search of the 'Promised Land', led in turn by Moses and Joshua. However, there is no agreement about their route. A recent suggestion offers an alternative to that on the map. It suggests that the Jews passed along the north coast, then crossed to Kadesh-Barnea, arriving at Mount Sinai, which rose above the limestone plain of Har Karkom.

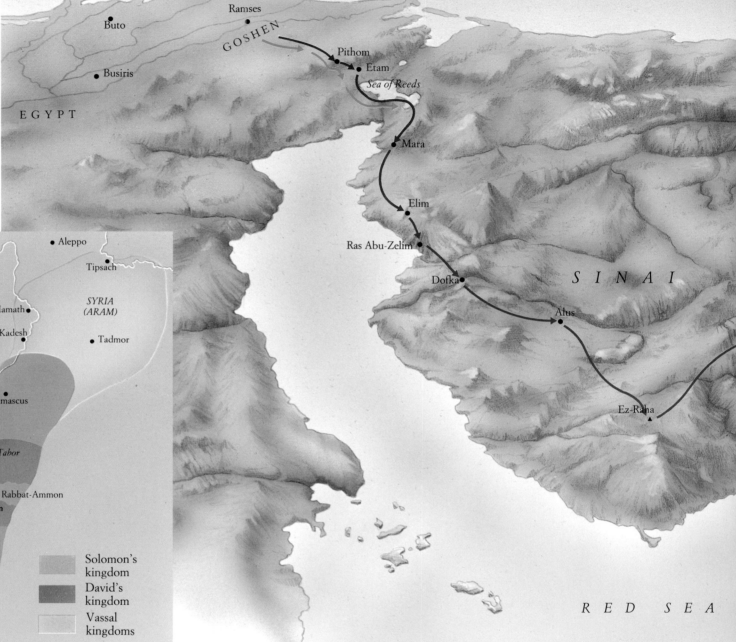

Ramses
Buto
Busiris
GOSHEN
Pithom
Etam
Sea of Reeds
EGYPT
Mara
Elim
Ras Abu-Zelim
Dofka
SINAI
Alus
Ez-Raha
RED SEA

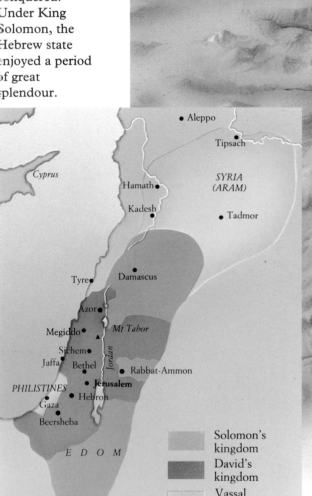

Aleppo
Tipsach
Cyprus
SYRIA (ARAM)
Hamath
Kadesh
Tadmor
Tyre
Damascus
Azor
Megiddo
Mt Tabor
Sichem
Jordan
Jaffa
Bethel
Rabbat-Ammon
PHILISTINES
Jerusalem
Gaza
Hebron
Beersheba
EDOM

Solomon's kingdom
David's kingdom
Vassal kingdoms

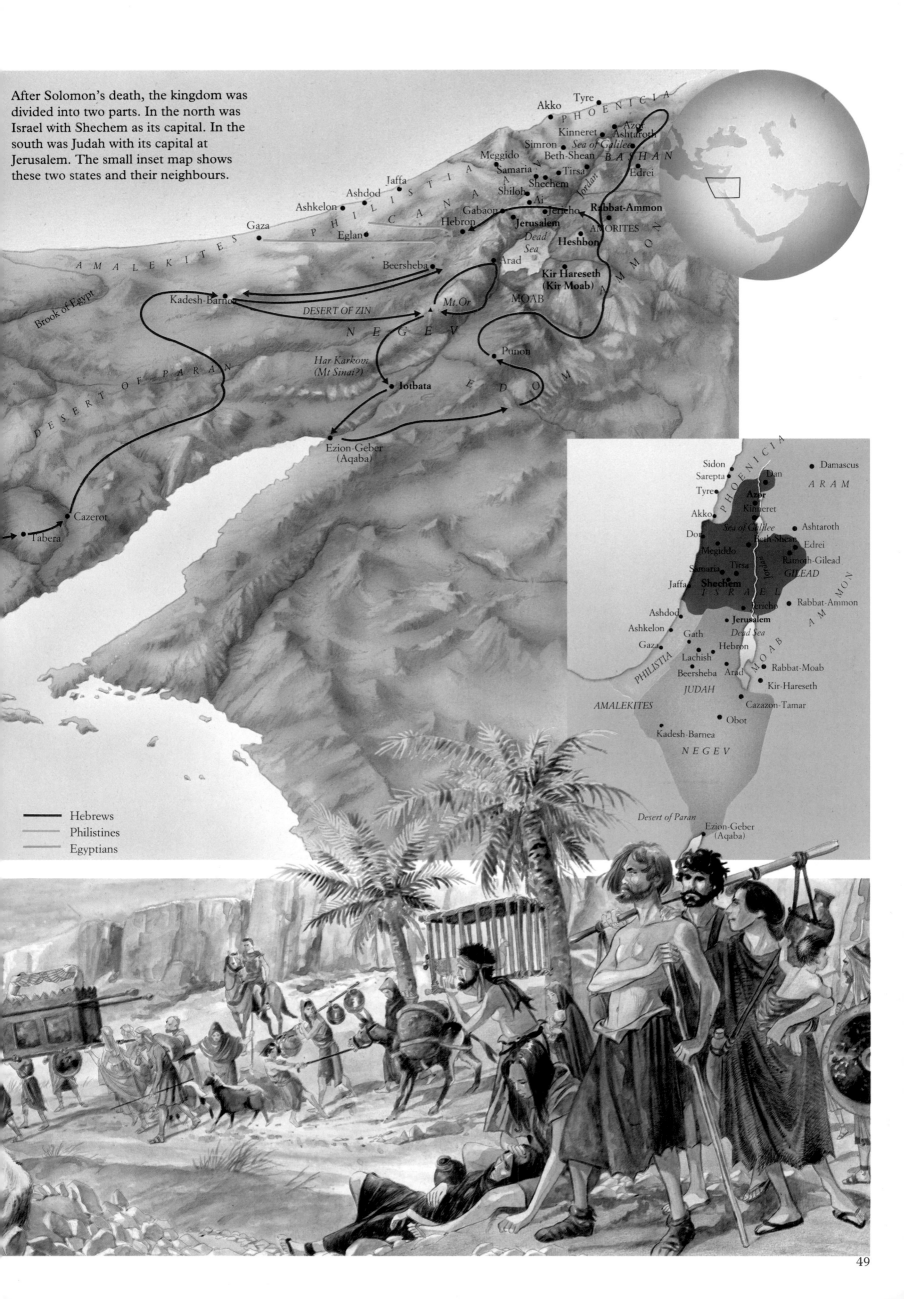

After Solomon's death, the kingdom was divided into two parts. In the north was Israel with Shechem as its capital. In the south was Judah with its capital at Jerusalem. The small inset map shows these two states and their neighbours.

Tyre
Akko
PHOENICIA
Kinneret
Azor
Ashtaroth
Simron
Sea of Galilee
BASHAN
Meggido
Beth-Shean
Samaria
Tirsa
Edrei
Shechem
Jordan
Shiloh
Ai
Ashdod
Jaffa
CANAAN
Jericho
Rabbat-Ammon
Ashkelon
Gabaon
Jerusalem
AMORITES
Gaza
Hebron
Dead
PHILISTIA
Eglan
Sea
Heshbon
AMMON
AMALEKITES
Arad
Kir Hareseth
Brook of Egypt
Beersheba
(Kir Moab)
Kadesh-Barnea
Mt. Or
MOAB
DESERT OF ZIN
NEGEV
Punon
Har Karkom
(Mt Sinai?)
Iotbata
EDOM
DESERT OF PARAN
Ezion-Geber
(Aqaba)
Cazerot
Tabera

Sidon
Damascus
Sarepta
Dan
PHOENICIA
ARAM
Tyre
Azor
Kinneret
Akko
Sea of Galilee
Ashtaroth
Dor
Beth-Shean
Edrei
Megiddo
Ramoth-Gilead
Samaria
Tirsa
GILEAD
Jaffa
ISRAEL
Shechem
Jordan
Ashdod
Jericho
Rabbat-Ammon
Ashkelon
Gath
Jerusalem
Gaza
Hebron
Dead Sea
Lachish
MOAB
Rabbat-Moab
Beersheba
Arad
Kir-Hareseth
JUDAH
Cazazon-Tamar
AMALEKITES
Obot
Kadesh-Barnea
NEGEV
Desert of Paran
Ezion-Geber
(Aqaba)

—— Hebrews
—— Philistines
—— Egyptians

49

12 THE BIRTH OF ISRAEL

In the Bible, the Book of Exodus tells how Moses, after the vision of a burning bush on Mount Sinai, or Hoveb (present-day Gebel Mûsa), led his people out of Egypt, where they had lived in slavery in the land of Goshen.

The exodus

The exodus began either in the last year of the pharaoh Ramses II, who ruled from 1290 to 1224 BC, or in the very first years of his heir, Merneptah, who was on the throne from 1224 to 1214 BC. In the Bible story, the caravan of 600,000 Israelites, consisting of about 600 families or clans, headed south, pursued by the pharaoh's chariots. They reached the Sea of Reeds (traditionally, but erroneously, translated as the Red Sea). This was a marshy area near the Gulf of Suez. Moses, instructed by God, led his people across the marsh. The heavy Egyptian chariots became bogged down and could not follow. The Israelites then went down the Sinai peninsula to Mount Sinai, though scholars do not know the precise location of the mountain described in the Bible.

Crossing the great limestone plain of Paran, the Israelites then reached Kadesh-Barnea. For about forty years, this remained the centre, from where the semi-nomadic tribes scattered along the slopes of Mount Or (Gebel Madheira), Negev and the area of Edom.

At the same time, much of the Near East was being devastated by periodic invasions of the Sea Peoples. The old fragmented city-states along the Syrian-Palestine coast had re-emerged, and with these the Israelite settlers were soon in conflict.

Joshua's wars

Avoiding the territories of the Moabites and Ammonites (descendants of Abraham's nephew, Lot), the Israelites went into Jordan and fought the peoples of Basan and Argob. According to the Book of Deuteronomy, Moses died while he was on Moabite territory. Joshua then took over as leader of the Israelites. At first his progress was slow. Then he made a breakthrough and secured possession of key points in the mountainous regions, which were safe for the nomadic tribes and rich in pastureland. Then Joshua conquered Jericho, Jordan and Ai, which opened the way to Canaan for the Israelites (Book of Joshua). Another victory at Gabaon over Adoni-Zedek, king of Jerusalem (where Joshua 'shut off the sun'), gave them possession of the southern regions. To the north, at the battle of the Waters of Merom, near Azor, the enemy was pushed back to the coast south of Tyre.

After these first conquests, between 1190 and 1150 BC, the Israelites allocated territories to the Twelve Tribes and cities to the priestly tribe of the Levites. This resulted in many conflicts with the peoples among whom the Israelites had settled (Book of Judges). There was also little cohesion among the tribes, and the attractions of new sophisticated but pagan cultures at times threatened the identity of 'God's people'. By the end of the 11th century BC, the Israelites were led by the Judges, charismatic but dictatorial

The exodus (pictured in colour on pages 48/49) as described in the Bible. After fleeing from slavery in Egypt, the Jews travelled over the sand dunes along the Sinai peninsula. The enormous caravan of refugees, glad of a plentiful water supply, remained encamped for about a year on the fertile plain dominated by Mount Horeb. This is where, according to the Bible, Moses received the Ten Commandments from God and where the Jews entered into a covenant (agreement) with God. The exodus had set the Israelites free. They now agreed to follow God's laws and live in unity as one nation.

They built a wooden chest, known as the Ark of the Covenant, seen being carried on poles in the centre of the picture, and a tabernacle to house the Ark and be a place of worship. This was a kind of portable tent. Like everything else, it had to be carried on the journey. After consecrating new priests, the Israelites marched north across the Paran desert, wandering for about forty years in the arid region of Kadesh-Barnea. The picture shows the Israelites on the march. Most are on foot. Their flocks go with them, and donkeys carry a few personal possessions.

THE BIBLE

The Bible has two main parts, called the Old Testament and the New Testament. The story of the ancient Israelites is told in the Old Testament, almost all of which was written in Hebrew (the rest was written in Aramaic). The New Testament (sacred only to Christians) tells of the life, work and death of Jesus, and the early spread of Christianity. The first five books of the Old Testament are called the Pentateuch. They contain the Law of Moses and are often known simply as the Torah (Law). They are Genesis, Exodus, Leviticus, Numbers and Deuteronomy. These books are followed by the historical books, which tell the history of the Jews after the death of Moses. They include all the books listed on this page. The remainder of the Old Testament includes the Books of Wisdom (containing Psalms, Proverbs and the Song of Solomon), the Prophets, and the Apocrypha, which was not part of the original Hebrew Bible.

JOSHUA
The Israelite invasion of Canaan led by Joshua, Moses' successor. **(c.1230-1200 BC)**

JUDGES
The turbulent history of the kingless period after Joshua's death. **(1200-1070 BC)**

RUTH
The story of the widowed Moabite girl who married Boaz during the period of the Judges.

SAMUEL
The rule of Israel's first kings, Saul and David, chosen by the prophet Samuel, and the uniting of Israel.

KINGS
Solomon's golden age, the division of the kingdom into Israel and Judah, the Babylonian invasion and Jerusalem's destruction. **(975-586 BC)**

CHRONICLES
Another history of God's people after Saul's death to Jerusalem's fall.

EZRA
The Jews' return from exile in Babylon and the rebuilding of the temple, led by Ezra.

NEHEMIAH
Religious reform and the rebuilding of Jerusalem's walls. **(445-433 BC)**

ESTHER
The story of the Jewish wife of the Persian king whose courage and faith saved her people from a massacre. **(5th century BC)**

leaders, who guided the tribes in the name of God. They organized resistance against the Moabites of Eglon, the Canaanites of Azor and the Ammonites of Galaad. Samson, acting more as an individual hero than a judge, started the uprising against the Philistines, who were one of the Sea Peoples.

King Saul

The lack of central power caused grave friction and civil wars among the tribes. This led to a long period of subjection to the Philistines, beginning in 1050 BC with the destruction of the sanctuary at Shiloh. The Ark of the Covenant, the Jews' most sacred object, fell into enemy hands and the responsibility for Israel's leadership was assumed by the judge-prophet Samuel. He was asked by the elders to choose a king, and he chose Saul.

In 1030 BC, Saul was consecrated as first king of Israel. In the twenty years of his rule, he fought against the Ammonites and Amalekites, and sought many times to stop the ruthless advance of the Philistines, who were penetrating deep into Judean territory, almost as far as Jerusalem.

David and Solomon

Saul died around 1010 BC, still fighting the Philistines. David, who had been exiled as a rebel, was elected king by the tribe of Judah and after a civil war with Abner, he became unchallenged king. He made Jerusalem his capital.

After David, his son Solomon ruled in peace for 40 years. He married the daughter of the Egyptian pharaoh, and had widespread trade links. After his death, the kingdom was again divided, in around 937 BC. Israel in the north was formed by ten tribes, with its capital first at Shechem, then at Samaria; Judah was formed by the tribes of Judah and Benjamin, with Jerusalem as its capital.

Divided, the Jews quarrelled and fell victim to outside attack. The Prophets predicted God's punishment for pagan practices, and the Assyrians of Tiglathpileser III (744-727 BC) were to be the instrument of God's anger. Tiglathpileser's son Shalmaneser conquered Samaria and destroyed Israel. Judah also collapsed, in 586 BC, when Nebuchadrezzar conquered Jerusalem and deported the Jews as slaves to Babylon.

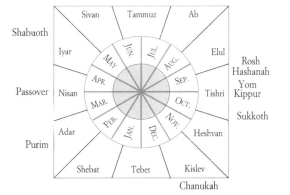

The Jewish year (above) is divided into twelve months, and marked by festivals recording ancient traditions. Rosh Hashanah, the Jewish New Year (which usually falls in September), celebrates the Creation and begins ten days of penitence ending with Yom Kippur, the Day of Atonement. Practising Jews spend this solemn day of fasting in the synagogue. Five days later comes Sukkoth, or Tabernacles, a harvest festival that gives thanks for God's protection of the Jews in the desert. The liberation by Judas Maccabeus and Dedication of the Temple in 165 BC is celebrated in a festival of lights called Chanukah (usually just before Christmas). Purim celebrates the deliverance of the Jews from Haman by the intercession of Esther. The festival of Pesach, or Passover (usually near Easter), celebrates the liberation of the Jews from slavery in Egypt. Seven weeks later, Shabuoth, the festival of Weeks, gives thanks to God for the harvest and the laws given to Moses in the desert.

A harp, similar to the instrument that David might have played during his youth when he spent long hours guarding his father's flocks.

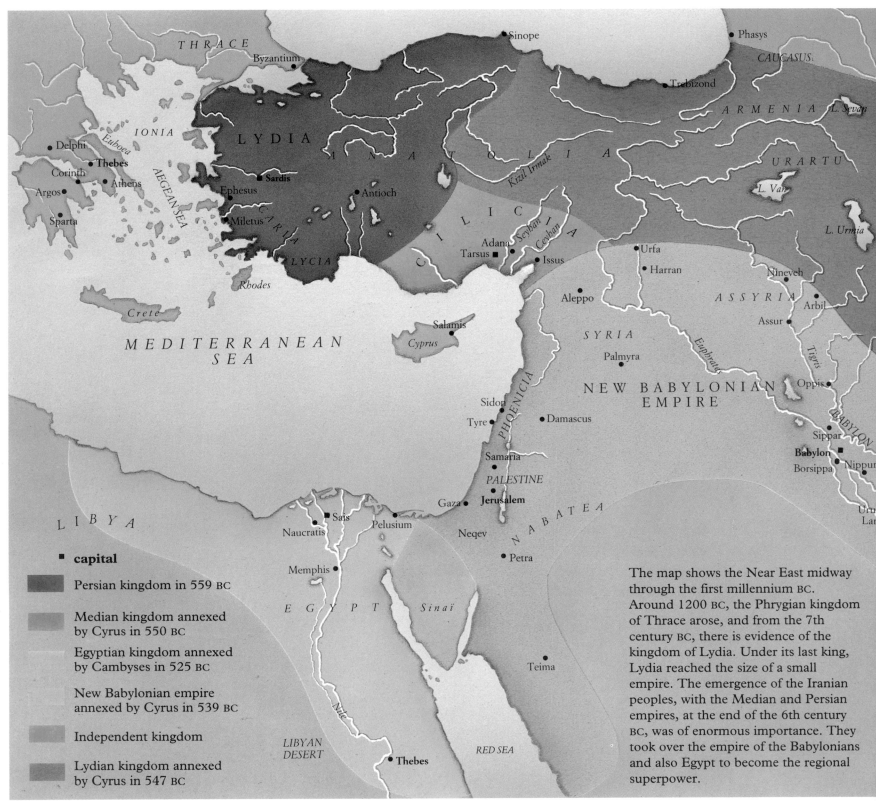

The map shows the Near East midway through the first millennium BC. Around 1200 BC, the Phrygian kingdom of Thrace arose, and from the 7th century BC, there is evidence of the kingdom of Lydia. Under its last king, Lydia reached the size of a small empire. The emergence of the Iranian peoples, with the Median and Persian empires, at the end of the 6th century BC, was of enormous importance. They took over the empire of the Babylonians and also Egypt to become the regional superpower.

Legend:

- ■ **capital**
- Persian kingdom in 559 BC
- Median kingdom annexed by Cyrus in 550 BC
- Egyptian kingdom annexed by Cambyses in 525 BC
- New Babylonian empire annexed by Cyrus in 539 BC
- Independent kingdom
- Lydian kingdom annexed by Cyrus in 547 BC

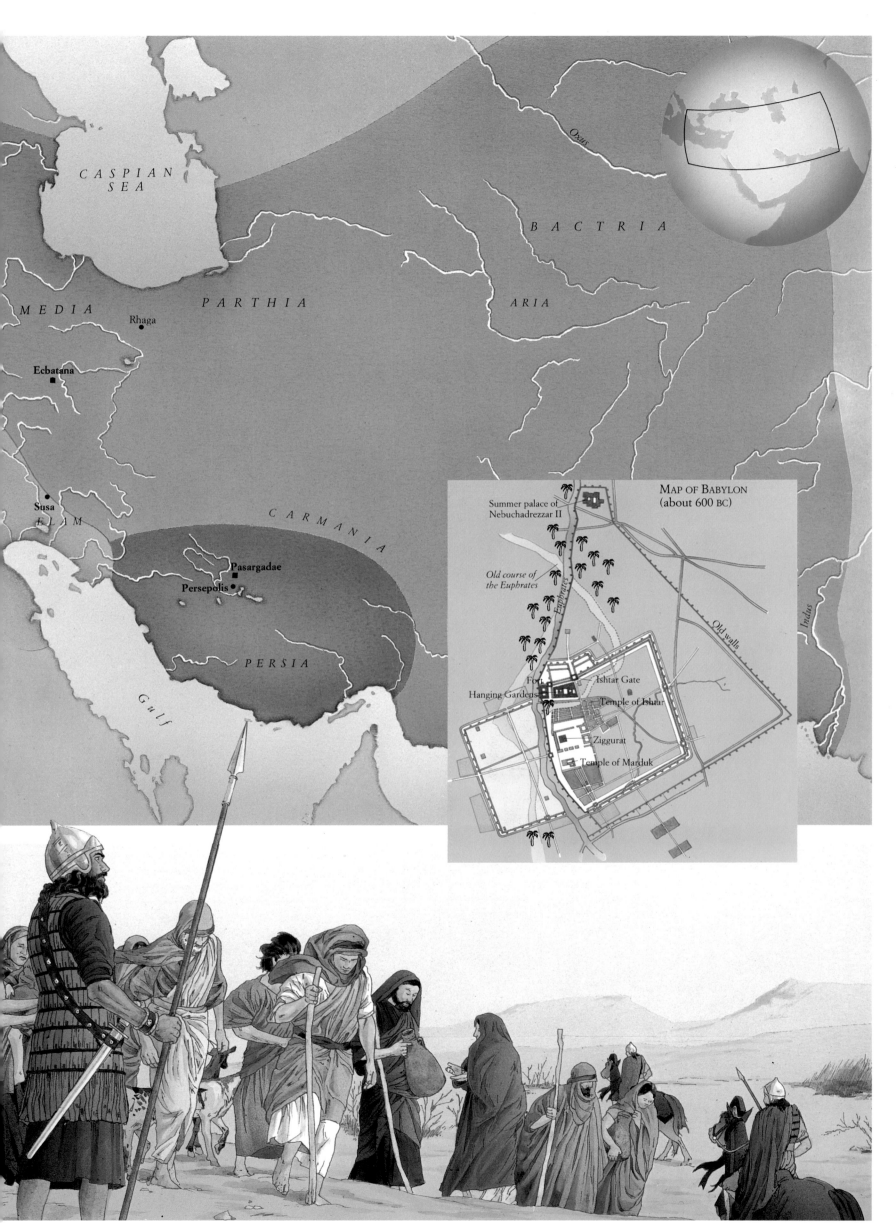

CASPIAN
SEA

BACTRIA

Oxus

MEDIA

PARTHIA

ARIA

Rhaga

Ecbatana

Susa
ELAM

CARMANIA

Pasargadae

Persepolis

PERSIA

Gulf

Indus

MAP OF BABYLON
(about 600 BC)

Summer palace of
Nebuchadrezzar II

*Old course of
the Euphrates*

Euphrates

Old walls

Fort

Ishtar Gate

Hanging Gardens

Temple of Ishtar

Ziggurat

Temple of Marduk

13 THE LAST EMPIRES

Assyria's grip on Mesopotamia lasted through the reigns of twenty-six kings, from the 10th century BC until the death of Assurbanipal in 627 BC. They belonged, it seems, to at least twenty-one different dynasties, made up of Chaldean tribal leaders, Assyrian kings and Babylonian princes. There followed a Babylonian revolt against the Assyrians. In 626 BC Nabopolassar, a Chaldean leader, gained power in Babylon. For ten years, he fought against the Assyrians until he controlled Babylonia (616 BC) and was able to march into the heart of the empire. In 614 BC, the Babylonians joined forces with the Medes. Taking advantage of Assyrian weakness, together they sacked Assur and, in 612 BC, conquered Nineveh. By 609 BC Assyrian resistance had ended.

A changing world

The fall of Assyria caused a chain reaction that changed the political geography of the Near East. The Egyptians, who had fought on the side of the Assyrians, tried to gain supremacy in the west. But they were hindered by Nebuchadrezzar II, son of Nabopolassar, who in 605 BC succeeded his father to lead the New Babylonian empire.

The Medians in the meantime, led by King Cyaxares, destroyer of Nineveh, invaded Anatolia. Crushing the kingdom of Urartu, they then fought a war lasting five years (590-585 BC) with the king of Lydia. Peace between the Lydians and Medians was mediated by Nebuchadrezzar, who had become the most powerful leader in the Middle East. Under a new king, Croesus, Lydia extended its domain to the Greek cities on the Aegean coast, but it, like Media, was absorbed by the emerging Persian Empire of Cyrus II who had inherited the throne of Persia in 559 BC.

Nebuchadrezzar II was now head of an empire, as great as Assyria's had been, and the second half of his reign was devoted to its organization. His mediation between the Lydians and Medians in 585 BC showed that he was adept

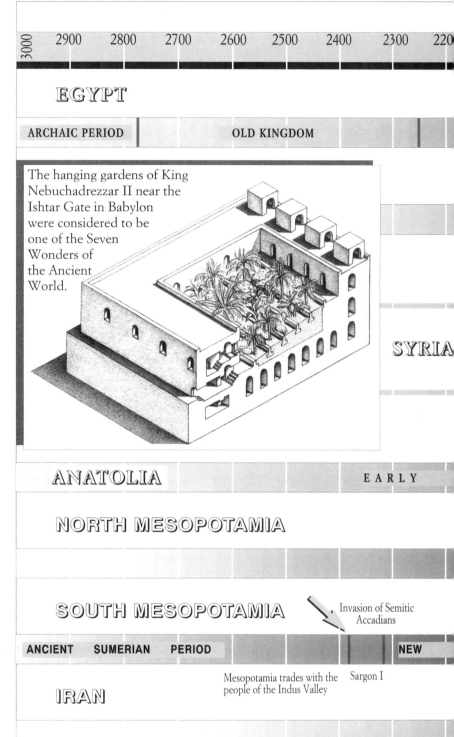

3000	2900	2800	2700	2600	2500	2400	2300	220

EGYPT

ARCHAIC PERIOD	OLD KINGDOM

The hanging gardens of King Nebuchadrezzar II near the Ishtar Gate in Babylon were considered to be one of the Seven Wonders of the Ancient World.

SYRIA

ANATOLIA
EARLY

NORTH MESOPOTAMIA

SOUTH MESOPOTAMIA
Invasion of Semitic Accadians

ANCIENT SUMERIAN PERIOD			NEW

Mesopotamia trades with the people of the Indus Valley · Sargon I

IRAN

Defeated Jews (pictured in colour on pages 50/51) are led as slaves to Babylon. Their captivity resulted from the expansionist politics of Nebuchadrezzar, who targeted Syria, Palestine and Egypt. According to his own description, 'the armies fought in an open field and inflicted defeat after defeat on each other'. In 597 BC King Joachim of Jerusalem, with many of his subjects, was deported to Babylon. When the Jews tried to rise up against Babylonian rule, their city of Jerusalem was attacked. The siege that followed lasted for more than a year until the city was taken and the inhabitants deported as slaves. The picture shows the captives, young and old, struggling across the desert, guarded by Babylonian soldiers. For the Jews, their Babylonian captivity lasted until 539 BC, when Cyrus of Persia conquered Babylon. Throughout this time of exile, the Jews held fast to their religious traditions, refusing to follow the cult of Marduk imposed by Nabonidus and his son Belshazzar. According to the Book of Daniel in the Bible, Belshazzar was killed after an irreverent banquet at which mysterious words of warning, written by an unknown hand, appeared as if by supernatural means on the wall.

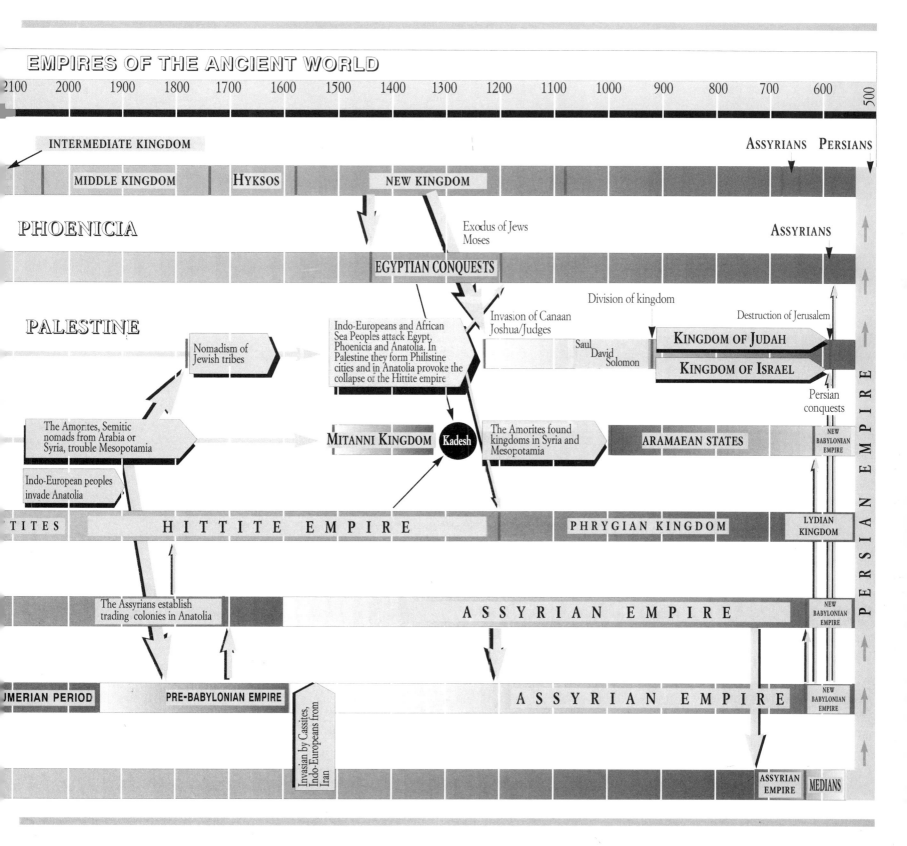

EMPIRES OF THE ANCIENT WORLD

2100 2000 1900 1800 1700 1600 1500 1400 1300 1200 1100 1000 900 800 700 600 500

INTERMEDIATE KINGDOM

ASSYRIANS PERSIANS

MIDDLE KINGDOM | HYKSOS | NEW KINGDOM

PHOENICIA

ASSYRIANS

Exodus of Jews
Moses

EGYPTIAN CONQUESTS

PALESTINE

Division of kingdom

Indo-Europeans and African Sea Peoples attack Egypt, Phoenicia and Anatolia. In Palestine they form Philistine cities and in Anatolia provoke the collapse of the Hittite empire

Invasion of Canaan
Joshua/Judges

Saul
David
Solomon

Destruction of Jerusalem

KINGDOM OF JUDAH

KINGDOM OF ISRAEL

Persian conquests

Nomadism of Jewish tribes

The Amorites, Semitic nomads from Arabia or Syria, trouble Mesopotamia

MITANNI KINGDOM | Kadesh

The Amorites found kingdoms in Syria and Mesopotamia

ARAMAEAN STATES

NEW BABYLONIAN EMPIRE

Indo-European peoples invade Anatolia

TITES | HITTITE EMPIRE

PHRYGIAN KINGDOM

LYDIAN KINGDOM

PERSIAN EMPIRE

The Assyrians establish trading colonies in Anatolia

ASSYRIAN EMPIRE

NEW BABYLONIAN EMPIRE

UMERIAN PERIOD | PRE-BABYLONIAN EMPIRE

Invasion by Cassites, Indo-Europeans from Iran

ASSYRIAN EMPIRE

NEW BABYLONIAN EMPIRE

ASSYRIAN EMPIRE | MEDIANS

at ensuring peaceful relations with his closest and most dangerous neighbours. Even so, he reinforced Babylon's defences by surrounding it with deep water moats and building a huge brick and bitumen-cemented wall between the Tigris and the Euphrates. Stones from all over the empire were brought in for these massive building works.

The Fall of Babylon

Nebuchadrezzar II died in 562 BC and for seven years there was rivalry among his relatives for the succession until Nabonidus (556-539 BC) was installed on the throne. He was a strong leader, but not related to the imperial family. He promoted the cult of the god Sin (Marduk) of Harran in Babylon, angering the priests of the Babylonian holy cities (Nibbur, Uruk, Babylon, Borsipa, Larsa and Ur). This religious quarrel hindered government. So Nabonidus moved to Taima in northwestern Arabia, leaving his son, Belshazzar, to rule in Babylon.

In 539 BC, Cyrus the Great, of Persia, moved against

Babylonia. He had already defeated Croesus in Lydia in 547 BC. Nabonidus was taken prisoner, and according to a later tradition, was made governor of Carmania (southern Iran) by Cyrus. Of Belshazzar there is no trace.

The New Babylonian empire was thereby ended. Cyrus the Great was famous, by his own account, for his benevolent rule. The Jews hailed him as a liberator who freed them from Babylonian tyranny and authorized them to build the Temple at Jerusalem. Babylon became the most splendid city of the Persian empire. Cyrus died in 530 BC and was buried at his capital, Pasargadae, in a simple stone tomb. Another king who earned the title 'Great', Alexander of Macedonia, had the tomb restored two hundred years later while he was ruling the kingdom founded by Cyrus. Cyrus was succeeded by Cambyses II (530-522 BC), who made Egypt into a Persian province in 525 BC.

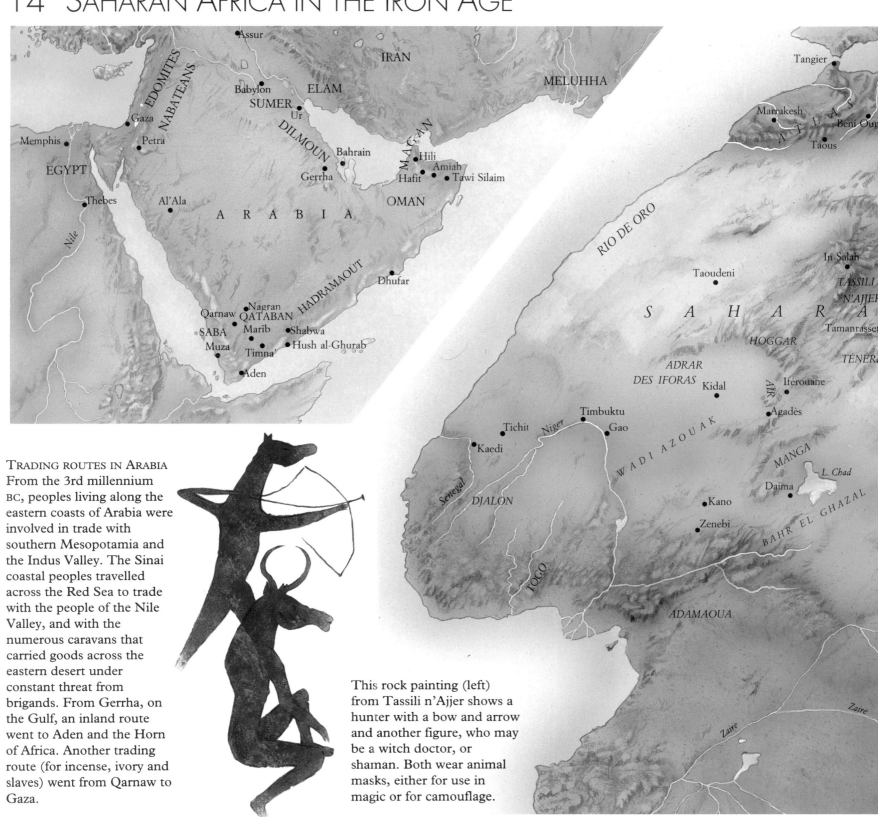

TRADING ROUTES IN ARABIA
From the 3rd millennium BC, peoples living along the eastern coasts of Arabia were involved in trade with southern Mesopotamia and the Indus Valley. The Sinai coastal peoples travelled across the Red Sea to trade with the people of the Nile Valley, and with the numerous caravans that carried goods across the eastern desert under constant threat from brigands. From Gerrha, on the Gulf, an inland route went to Aden and the Horn of Africa. Another trading route (for incense, ivory and slaves) went from Qarnaw to Gaza.

This rock painting (left) from Tassili n'Ajjer shows a hunter with a bow and arrow and another figure, who may be a witch doctor, or shaman. Both wear animal masks, either for use in magic or for camouflage.

BIG GAME HUNTERS, UNFAMILIAR WITH THE BOW, BEFORE 8000 BC. ✳ PEOPLE FISHING AND GATHERING, USING BOWS AND POISONED ARROWS, FROM 8000 BC. ✳ CATTLE

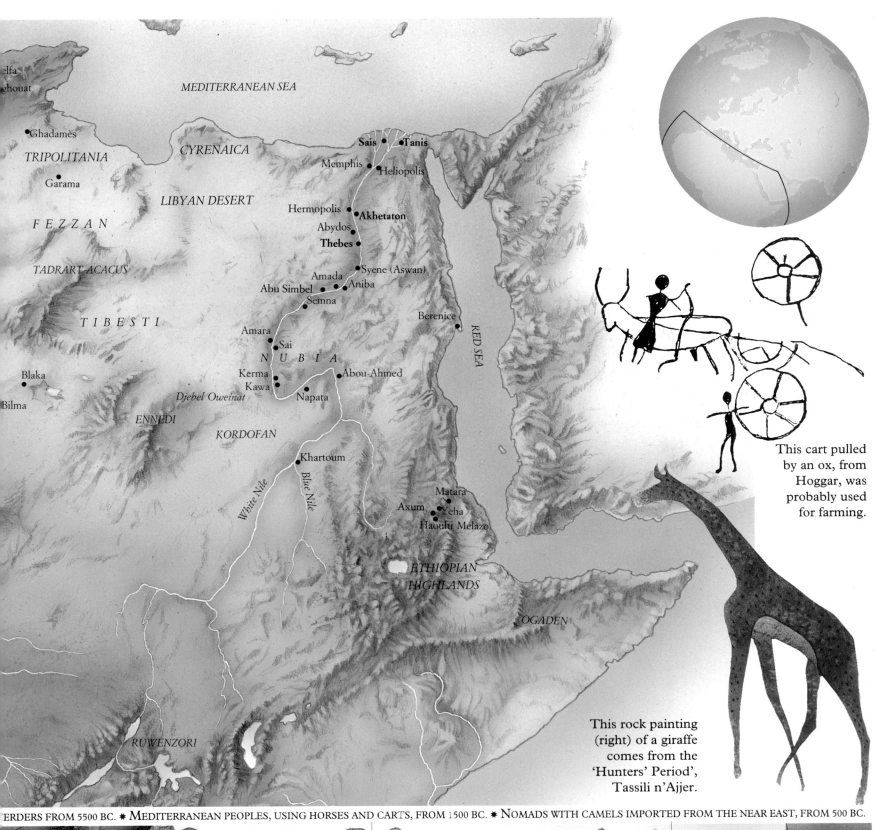

This cart pulled by an ox, from Hoggar, was probably used for farming.

This rock painting (right) of a giraffe comes from the 'Hunters' Period', Tassili n'Ajjer.

ERDERS FROM 5500 BC. ✷ MEDITERRANEAN PEOPLES, USING HORSES AND CARTS, FROM 1500 BC. ✷ NOMADS WITH CAMELS IMPORTED FROM THE NEAR EAST, FROM 500 BC.

14 SAHARAN AFRICA IN THE IRON AGE

A chariot pulled by two horses at a gallop. Like all the pictures on these two pages, this is a relief from the rock paintings at Tassili n'Ajjer.

Running men

Towards the end of the 3rd millennium BC, climatic changes brought about the complete drying up of the Sahara. No longer a fertile region, it became isolated from neighbouring cultures and declined. During this period, however, North Africa developed strong trading links with southern Spain. There was also brisk trade between Cyrenaica, Sicily, Sardinia, Malta and southern Italy.

Peoples of the interior

Around the springs of Fezzan and other oases, and along the Atlantic coast of the Sahara, people settled whom the Greeks called Ethiopians ('burnt faces'). They led a peaceful existence devoted not only to hunting and gathering but also to animal-rearing and farming using simple irrigation methods.

In the 13th and 12th centuries BC, the warlike Sea Peoples tried several times to invade Egypt and establish themselves throughout the Mediterranean. Among these invaders were the Libyans. In Egyptian pictures they are shown adorned with two long feathers or horned animal masks. Similar people appear in the rock paintings of the Sahara. Probably, the Libyans invaded the central Sahara from Cyrenaica, occupying in turn Tassili, Hoggar, Adrar des Iforas, and finally Aïr. In all these areas they replaced the original inhabitants, who at this time were mainly stock-rearing herders, who were pushed southwards by the arid climate in search of water and grazing. From the impregnable desert shelters, which had protected their predecessors for over twenty centuries, the newcomers made the Sahara the centre of a wide network trading in gold, salt and copper.

Wagons across the desert

There is evidence of many stopping-places along the Saharan trade routes. Many of these are found where rivers originating south of the Sahara flow into the Mediterranean Sea, places where water was always available. The whole area is marked by hundreds of rock paintings of wagons of the period between 1200 BC (the date of the Libyan and Sea Peoples' attack against Egypt) and the beginning of Christianity. The 'wagon trains' left tracks throughout the Sahara. The study of the paintings and the impressions left by the wagon wheels give clues to the methods and timing of people's progress through the region.

In the eastern Sahara there are traces of an inland route leading to different points on the coast, where there may have been landing places for ships. Evidence for this inland route comes from the remains of wagons found in Tamanart, south of Marrakesh, and of tracks found at Taous that

The scene (pictured in colour on pages 56/57) shows how the landscape of Tassili n'Ajjer has altered with the climatic changes of the past ten thousand years. As the Sahara became drier, human beings had to adapt their activities to suit a harsher environment. Where once hunters and gatherers could find plenty to eat, or herders find grazing, there is now only sand, except at oases or irrigated areas.

From the 8th millennium BC, North-central Africa experienced exceptional environmental changes, which rapidly turned green land into desert. The last Ice Age, which had covered northern Europe with ice, was followed by a period of great humidity, which in Africa produced the 'Green Sahara'. Vast areas now covered in bare rock and sand were then occupied by lakes or swamps, beside which people settled. Their civilization is recorded in the huge numbers of rock drawings and paintings that decorate caves and ravines all over the Sahara.

About six thousand years ago, the region began to dry up. People clung to areas where there were springs or moved closer to shrinking lakes or settled along the Nile or in wadis, such as Fayum, which caught the periodic floodwaters of the great river.

Warrior with
sword, spear
and shield

Marching soldiers

Ostrich

Pair of gazelles

form a continuous trail. Another route went round the Sirte coast, across Lake Chad, to stop at Tibesti, where there are further traces of wagons.

The most difficult route was across the central Sahara. This involved crossing Tassili n'Ajjer, a rugged and dangerous tableland with deep canyons. These dried-up river valleys, or wadis, the most well known of which was Fadnoun, probably had pathways through them. There were also a few larger, more open, valleys such as Tadjerdjert, through which Tassili could be crossed from north to south.

The array of wagon paintings in Tassili shows, however, that the most frequently used route was the east-west trail, where fifty-five individual wagons, or chariots, are painted in 'flying gallop' style. Some paintings show palm trees with date-pickers scaling the trunks. This indicates that there was a proper settlement, not just a temporary stopping-place.

Wars and trade

There is evidence that the Saharan wagons contained some warlike features, so perhaps the takeover of the interior of the Sahara was not all peaceful. Many later historians (Herodotus, Pliny, Strabo) suggest that, as well as the Libyans, there were other warlike peoples from the interior who used horses to pull war chariots and oxen to pull carts carrying goods. These well-armed people occupied Tassili and Hoggar, and forced the 'Ethiopian' peoples at the oases to retreat south to Niger.

Salt played a key role in the Saharan economy. There were rock-salt mines in the area, and the mining and trading of this valuable commodity, used for preserving and flavouring food, was immensely important. From the end of the 5th century BC, a Saharan trade system existed that was to remain in use for the next 2,000 years. Desert salt was sent to sub-Saharan Africa in exchange for gold, ivory and precious woods.

In this battle scene, soldiers carry round shields and spears. There are three people in the chariot, one on horseback. Three dogs join in the fight.

Men climbing palm trees to pick dates

Hippopotamus

GLOSSARY

The Nile provided plenty of fish and waterfowl for the Egyptians. These pictures, from the Old Kingdom period, show harpoon fishing from a reed boat (left) and a method of trapping birds with a net (right).

Alluvial Describes a deposit of sediment left behind by floodwaters in a river valley or over its flood plain.

Anarchy Disorder resulting from insufficient or no government.

Annexation Union of one state, or part of a state, with another state, either by conquest or agreement.

Archaic An early period in a civilization or in art.

Autonomy Self-government.

Basalt Rock formed by solidification of flowing liquid lava from a volcano.

Bas-relief Type of sculpture in which the figures are slightly raised from a flat surface.

Bureaucracy Government by a central administration, or the civil servants or officials who run a country.

Captivity Imprisonment; the 'Babylonian captivity' describes the slavery of the Jews in the city of Babylon.

Cartouche An oval ring bearing a pharaoh's name and other titles in hieroglyphics.

Cataract A sudden change in level of a river bed, causing a waterfall. The cataracts of the Nile made navigation between different stretches of the river impossible.

Chalcolithic The period between the Neolithic (New Stone Age) and the Bronze Age, when copper was first used.

City-state A city that is also an independent state and holds sway over the surrounding area.

Civil war Armed struggle between citizens of the same state for political or social reasons.

Coalition League or alliance of states and people with a common military or political goal.

Code List of laws or rules.

Cult System of religious worship, with its own rules and ceremonies.

Cuneiform Wedge-shaped writing of Akkad and Sumeria.

Dagger Short sword with a double-edged blade.

Deportation Banishment or forced movement of a person or persons from their home or country.

Dignitary High-ranking official who by birth or personal merit attains responsibility.

Drainage Reclaiming wetland for farming by draining water away in canals, ditches and pipes.

Dynasty Succession of rulers from the same family, in a direct line from the founder. In Egypt there were 31 dynasties.

Epic Narrative story or poem celebrating the deeds of one or more heroes, who may personify the national character.

Exodus Migration, or mass departure from a place, especially the flight of the Jews from Egypt, led by Moses, which is described in the Book of Exodus in the Bible.

Federation Union of self-governing states, each with its own laws, but subject to a central government.

Fertile Describes land that is good for growing crops.

Fertile Crescent Region in the Middle East, from Palestine to Iran, that has a crescent shape on the map. Here, around 9000-7000 BC, farming started.

Hierarchy Order of importance or rank of people in a group.

Hieroglyphics Ancient Egyptian writing made up of picture- and sound-symbols.

Historical cycle Period of time with marked political, social and economic similarities.

Ideography Writing system representing ideas by symbols (ideograms) rather than signs corresponding to sounds.

Lapis lazuli Hard blue semi-precious stone, beautiful azure-blue in colour, used for jewellery or decoration.

Levantine Referring to the Levant, the eastern part of the Mediterranean, from southeastern Anatolia to Egypt.

Limestone Type of sedimentary rock used for building. Marble is a form of limestone that has been hardened by heat and pressure underground.

Lower Egypt Northern part of the Nile valley near the delta. In the time of the pharaohs, it was the area from Memphis to the Mediterranean coast.

Mesopotamia Land between the Tigris and Euphrates rivers, where modern Iraq is.

Metamorphic Describes rock that has been changed by natural forces from one form into another.

Myrrh Perfumed resin, reddish-brown in colour, which seeps from some Arabian and African tree-barks. It is used in perfumery and pharmacy.

Necropolis A burial area; the word is Greek for 'city of the dead'.

Neolithic The New Stone Age, a period characterized by farming, working with polished stone tools, and the invention of pottery.

Nomad People with no permanent homes who wander in search of grazing for their sheep, goats, horses- or other animals.

Oasis Waterhole in the desert.

Obsidian Hard, glassy, black volcanic rock, used for making tools.

Pharaoh King of Egypt. The title was not used until the 18th Dynasty (1500s BC).

Pictography Primitive form of writing in which ideas and objects are shown in pictures.

Proto Prefix meaning 'before' in time and space. Protodynastic, for example, means 'before the introduction of dynasties'.

Seal Engraved stone or metal cylinder used to stamp an image or decorative motif on soft clay or wax.

Secular Belonging to a lay, or non-religious, society.

Semitic Describes the Semitic family of languages, including Akkadian, Phoenician, Ugarite, Hebrew and Aramaic, Arabic and Ethiopian. Semitic peoples share linguistic and cultural origins, though they are not physically alike.

Site Place where archaeological studies are carried out into buildings, tombs, roads and other features that once were there.

Slinger Soldier armed with a sling-shot or catapult for hurling stones.

Stele Inscribed stone slab or monument, perhaps commemorating a dead ruler or announcing a law.

Stylize To represent something, such as a person or animal, by simplifying its features and reducing them to essential details in a picture.

Tablet Small block of clay used mainly in Mesopotamia for writing. Once fired, the hard clay preserved the writing.

Tell Small hill made from layers of old building remains, one on top of the other.

Tribal Describes a tribe or group of related families, usually under a chief.

Tribute Tax, paid in money or in kind (goods or crops), imposed by a ruler on individual subjects or community.

Tyrian purple Purple-red dye obtained from certain molluscs. The Phoenicians produced highly-valued cloth with this dye.

Upper Egypt Southern part of the Nile valley, closest to the river's source. In the time of the pharaohs, it was the region between the first cataract and the city of Memphis.

Urban Describes the city or city life.

Vassal A slave or servant. A vassal state was one bound to obey a greater power, such as an empire.

Wadi Dried-up river-bed typical of the Sahara and other African deserts.

Ziggurat Temple building, like an artificial mountain or pyramid, built in Mesopotamia.

INDEX